MIRACLES

Around the

Globe

MIRACLES
Around the
Globe

Dale Van Steenis

Pleasant W rd
A Division of WINEPRESS PUBLISHING

Printed in the United States of America

Packaged by Pleasant Word, a division of WinePress Publishing, PO Box 428, Enumclaw, WA 98022. The views expressed or implied in this work do not necessarily reflect those of Pleasant Word, a division of WinePress Publishing. Ultimate design, content, and editorial accuracy of this work are the responsibilities of the author.

Unless otherwise noted, all Scriptures are taken from the Holy Bible, New International Version, Copyright © 1973, 1978, 1984 by the International Bible Society. Used by permission of Zondervan Publishing House. The "NIV" and "New International Version" trademarks are registered in the United States Patent and Trademark Office by International Bible Society.

Scripture references marked KJV are taken from the King James Version of the Bible.

Scripture references marked NASB are taken from the New American Standard Bible, © 1960, 1963, 1968, 1971, 1972, 1973, 1975, 1977 by The Lockman Foundation. Used by permission.

ISBN 1-57921-612-9
Library of Congress Catalog Card Number: 2003101571

TABLE OF CONTENTS

Chapter 1

GOD IS AT WORK

A lifetime of travel and ministry around the world has made my life, and that of my family, inestimably richer. I have lodged in castles and coops, eaten pâté and perch, slept on boards and beds of silk. Conversations have been held with lepers and leaders in high government offices, with commanders, commissars, and Communists. I have been in president's offices and visited peasants, shepherds in their fields, and nuns. I have traveled by first class international airlines and rickshaws. Donkey carts and the most modern trains have carried me from place to place. I have been enriched by talking with church leaders at every level and of many kinds across the world. Ministry has been in houses, sheds, out-of-doors, tents, exposition grounds, theaters, opera and movie houses, and churches both grand and plain. From this rich background of experience has come a selection of stories clearly showing God at work.

Get ready to have your spirit lifted and your faith raised a notch. The stories that follow are proof that *God is at work in the world today!*

Dale Van Steenis

PART ONE:

Miracles In Eastern Europe

$\mathscr{C}hapter$ 2

SALVATION AND SUFFERING

Author's note:

For many years I have had the privilege of traveling to many nations of the world, including the old Soviet Union and its former satellites. During the extreme Communist years, government restrictions and persecution were oppressive and frequent. Simply said, the government was against all forms of religious practice and used the police and KGB (secret police) to enforce its will. This story is about a humble man named Sergei, and his story is typical of dozens I have heard. The reader should remember that in the Stalin years, approximately 2 million believers were detained and disappeared in notoriously cruel places such as Magadan and Yurkata, both the sites of crematoriums used to dispose of persons. Many went to the crematoriums alive. In total, between so-called "religious" and "political" prisoners, millions of people were killed at the hands of their own government. The fact that Sergei survived is, by itself, a miracle.

Sergei's story is one of great personal grief and triumph. My life is richer for having met and fellowshiped with him.

As a young boy, Sergei was competitive. He loved all types of sports and liked to win. In winter he kicked the soccer ball indoors, practiced pitching baseball with a friend, wrestled, and generally kept the house in disorder with his activities.

The family lived in a manufacturing city in the U.S.S.R. Both mother and father worked as supervisors in a factory. Together, they earned about one-third more than the average factory laborers. Because of the extra income, the family enjoyed more pleasantries of life than most people in the city. They had a good apartment and, despite the Soviet system, life was reasonably good. The entire family went to the Black Sea for a month every year—a much-anticipated time.

Sergei's competitive spirit served him well in school and sports. Ultimately his good performances secured admission at the university. After some years at the university he completed his studies. Two weeks after graduation he was married to Nadja, a young lady he had met near the beginning of his college years.

Sergei and Nadja both worked in a large factory and held good positions. Life was good. But then Sergei began to drink, heavily at times, with his peers from work. In seven years he and his wife had three sons. The increased pressure and responsibilities at home and on the job produced more drinking and longer and more frequent pub stops. His marriage began to suffer, and arguments became more frequent.

One of Sergei's superiors had been watching him for some time. Zarad was known to be a man of few words, with quiet wisdom, and kindness—a rare type of person in a high position during the Communist days. Zarad could see Sergei's life unraveling. While at the same time, Sergei had noticed that Zarad was not to be seen in the beer halls and pubs. Occasionally Sergei wondered why Zarad was like that, separate and yet approachable. Why was this man different? What caused the touch of mystery around him?

One warm spring day Zarad invited Sergei to walk with him at lunchtime. While they were walking, Zarad explained that at one time his life was headed downward, exactly as Sergei's, because he had become an alcoholic. His children had learned to hate him, and he and his wife fought incessantly. One day, in the midst of this troubled lifestyle, their housekeeper explained that prayer and Bible study had changed her life and that of her family. To share this information was very dangerous for the housekeeper. She could have been both fired and jailed for doing so. The possession of a Bible or being known as a Christian brought certain arrest, fines, and lengthy jail sentences.

But the fear of that did not silence the woman. She gave Zarad and his wife a Gospel of John, urged them to read it, and told them to try to pray. They followed her instructions and God did come to them. He delivered Zarad of his alcoholism. For several years, the Gospel of John was the only scripture Zarad and his wife had to sustain them spiritually. There were no churches in their town. Group gatherings of Christians were "underground." The housekeeper occasionally prayed with the family, but not often. She never mentioned other Christians in the town.

So, Sergei discovered, it was faith in God that had changed Zarad. That was the reason he was not in the pubs and did not "hang out with the guys" after work. He had been delivered from alcoholism by faith in God. Sergei knew Zarad shared this story with him at great personal risk. He also gave him a Bible. Sergei, knowing he needed help, reached out for the Bible and for the fellowship Zarad offered.

After a few months, Sergei came to faith in Christ. The change was gradual but substantive. Wonderfully, the power that alcohol had over his life was broken. His behavior changed, as well as his family life. Such changes did not go unnoticed by his peers at work. Many of his friends had drinking and drug problems, and Sergei had encouraged many of them to party in prior days.

One of his friends, Andrei, a full-blown alcoholic, had separated from his wife and moved in with a barmaid from a local pub. Andrei could not figure out what had happened to Sergei. It didn't make sense to him. He constantly baited Sergei to resume his "party" lifestyle, but without success. Finally, Sergei decided to testify to Andrei as Zarad had to him. He wanted to help his friend out of his distressful lifestyle.

During a lunchtime chat in a city park, Sergei shared how the Lord had changed his life through prayer, Bible study, and a relationship with Jesus Christ. Andrei could hardly believe his good friend could believe in God, religion, and all that "stuff." He became angry and stormed off cursing. Sergeis' heart dropped and fear swept over him. If his comments became public, or were spoken near the wrong person, the secret police would be around to see him within days.

That is precisely what happened. Sergei's factory was large, and the government had placed an officer there whose task it was to teach and enforce Communist ideology. The man had the political power to see to it that everyone complied "or else." This enforcer was part and parcel of the dreaded KGB and had direct links to the local and federal police and the military. No one knows for sure, but it is highly likely that Andrei was the one who spoke to the officer since he was the only person to whom Sergei had entrusted the personal information about his life and conversion. No one else except Zarad knew his story. When the officer began to interrogate Sergei and threatened his job and family and life, Sergei answered all questions truthfully.

Two nights after the first interrogation, Sergei was arrested in the middle of the night, taken from his house, wrenched from the arms of his weeping wife. He was brought before a military officer, immediately declared guilty of "ideological crimes" against the state, and sentenced to life imprisonment at hard labor. The next morning he was sent by prison train to Siberia to serve out this harsh sentence.

During the first weeks of his imprisonment, the KGB repeatedly visited his house looking for Bibles and religious literature. They quizzed Sergei's wife about the couple's "religious" activities. They intimidated her with threats of government reprisals if she continued as a practicing Christian. There were no limits to their cruelty and harassment.

In the Siberian prison, Sergei was told that his wife had become a prostitute in the streets to earn money for her family. No letters or communications from his family were allowed to reach him. At home, Nadja was told, through an official letter, that Sergei had been killed in the midst of a prison riot he was accused of starting. Such barbarism and emotional torment was commonplace in the Communist years. Of course, neither story was true, but how were Nadja and Sergei to know?

Unbeknown to either Nadja or Sergei, Nadja was pregnant when Sergei was arrested and taken away. Because of the tremendous pressures brought upon her, and also because of some underlying medical problems, she died a few days after the birth of their fourth son. This news was kept from Sergei thousands of miles away in a Russian gulag.

Years went by until a time towards the end of the presidency of Mikhail Gorbechev, when the Russian authorities needed finances and better relationships with the West. Quietly, they began to release "religious" prisoners, among them Sergei. He returned to his home without notice just as he had been taken away.

The prison train arrived in Sergei's city and he was released. He headed straight for his former home and a long-awaited reunion with his wife and his children. He was shocked to learn from his cousin that his wife had died in childbirth and that all the stories told him about her by the prison authorities were false. For the first time, Sergei met his ten-year-old son, the boy he had fathered but had never met.

The news of a dead wife and an additional son was shocking to Sergei—as was the fact that his government had lied to him and kept him from communicating with his family. Would he respond to the injustices he had experienced? Would he become bitter and revengeful? Or would he be grateful for freedom, a new son, and the years of blessed marriage shared? Would he savor them as a sweet memory, and go on with life? Sergei had to make a choice.

As I heard this story over a long lunch in a small Russian city, I could feel my own anger begin to blaze. I asked Sergei if he could not find the people who perpetrated all these horrible things against him and take his revenge. Where was Andrei who obviously had tipped the authorities to Sergei's conversion?

"Andrei had frozen to death three winters before after falling down drunk in a blizzard," he told me. "He never woke up and was found three days later by a friend."

"But what about the authorities?" I asked. "Can't you bring cases against them in public court and be joined by many others who were similarly treated?"

Sergei's answer was a gentle rebuke to me and the heated emotions I was experiencing.

"I only told you this story because you asked," he said gently. "Normally, I do not speak about these things because now we have freedom to preach the gospel. Brother, let's not spend time on yesterday's problems. We have today and we can preach the gospel freely. Think of my blessings. I survived the gulag in Siberia. My wife is in heaven. I have a new son. And we have freedom now to tell people about Jesus. Let's use the time and opportunity to preach the gospel and not waste time thinking backwardly."

Tears flowed. I can tell you my heart was deeply affected by Sergei's demeanor and attitude. Godly men allow heavy trials to make them better. Lesser men become bitter. Today Sergei is a leading evangelist and church planter in his country. I'm sure his heart of forgiveness has touched many as it did mine.

Chapter 3

COMMISSIONED COURIER

I n and around Moscow, police and KGB pressure on religious groups and cell churches based in homes was increasing both in number and in severity of punishment. Sometimes the KGB would break up house meetings, take everyone's name and address, intimidate the people with threats regarding "illegal gatherings," and then take their leave. Things had changed. Now everyone, including older women and young mothers, were being arrested and detained. Most women were out of jail in three or four days, but the men were confined for a minimum of a month. None were allowed legal representation or visitors.

Eventually most were released, but a few were detained for indeterminate periods. There was never an answer as to why or when. It was during these arbitrary jail stays that the police and KGB would create their cases against the Christians. A few prisoners disappeared and were never heard from again. They probably died in the gulags of

Yurkata or Magadan in the Far East, or they died from being tortured.

These Christians were not arrested for theft, murder, or conspiracy against their government. They were arrested for meeting with a few other believers to read the Bible and pray. They were imprisoned for loving a God the state claimed did not exist. These things have happened not only in the Lenin-Stalin periods, but under every Russian leader since, including Gorbachev. All Soviet regimes have been repressive and bloody to one degree or another.

During one late night purge, ten leaders of the underground church movement were arrested and imprisoned. Their families were told the KGB wanted $25,000 in United States dollars (USD) to obtain their release. There were never any guarantees the church leaders would not be arrested again, but at least momentarily, if they paid, they would be able to rejoin their families and friends.

Where could Christians in Moscow get $25,000 USD? Most were poor. All their lives and jobs had been disrupted by jail terms and arrests and detainment from one night to several days. Few had enough to eat properly. Getting $25,000 USD was out of the question. To make this request even more ridiculous, it was illegal for Russians to possess foreign currency and to convert rubles to another currency (although it was done every day by the Communists and black marketers).

A person who did have dollars or German D-marks in his possession could buy anything. And there were no questions from the sellers if the buyer had "hard" currency— those from the wealthiest western nations. Dollars and D-marks were preferred.

Visitors came from the West from time to time to encourage the believers. Their visits had to be carefully planned so they did not arouse suspicion and the attention of the police. All meetings were held in secret. Often several cars were used, with the visitors, switching from one to another to escape detection. The route to the meeting place was always secret and circuitous. All meetings were held at night in the city. Much effort was expended to be sure no one was followed, as all Westerners usually were. Plans had to be carefully thought out and even more carefully executed.

There was a communication system, based on word-of-mouth, through which information traveled quickly all over Russia and also to the West. The message about the ten brothers who had been arrested was received in the West about one week later. The message said the money was desperately needed. Could anything be done? Word came back that a plan was being prepared and the families and other believers should simply pray to understand what the plan would be. Their understanding would be based on prayer alone.

The plan involved a young German couple who had studied in Russia and were fluent in the language. There were to go to Moscow on a "holiday" and would visit the opera, circus, museums, and other points of interest. But all these visits were really being made to arrange a point at which money for the prisoners could be transferred without being noticed.

Gerd and Jo signed up for the "Moscow Surprise Tour"—a week in and around Moscow with full sightseeing. They were to carry $25,000 USD with them for the pastors. The plan was very risky as first. Carrying that amount of money was a capital offense punishable by a prison term. Secondly, the "tourists" were depending on a "chance" meeting with a brother or sister so the money could be transferred without notice of the KGB or police. Gerd and Jo could not go to anyone's home or workplace, neither did they have any local addresses or names of believers. They did have the money though. It was taped in a small indented portion of Gerd's lower back.

The tour was in winter, so wearing bulky layers of clothing was the norm. But the ability to act casual and nonchalant was essential. After all, Gerd and Jo were on vacation. They were "tourists" and needed to act accordingly. Fortunately, both of them were skilled in the art of drama.

From one tourist point to another they went sightseeing. Surveillance levels were unusually high. It was always bad, but in Moscow during this trip it seemed stifling. The KGB agents were everywhere and at all times, doing their usual ridiculously predictable sleuthing: leaning in doorways at night with sunglasses on, standing behind trees hoping to pick up conversations, sitting in the hotel lobby reading a week-old daily paper, and so forth. Most of the time they were not hard to spot. They made it clear they were there.

Gerd and Jo had taken the train to Moscow because there were no X-ray machines used on the baggage and generally less thorough inspections. The transfer money had been carefully prepared by soaking it in water and shaping it into a packet to fit exactly into the depression in Gerd's lower back. It was virtually undetectable under the winter clothing. By traveling with a tour group and by train, they would not be inspected as closely.

Success. They arrived in Moscow without difficulty. In the midst of the on-off-the-bus and see-all-the-wonderful-sights of touring, they were constantly looking for the proper eye contact, the sense of knowing without speaking, the returned look of confirmation. Five of seven days passed and there was no contact with any brothers, just a herd of KGB "trailers" watching them and following them everywhere. The phone in their room was bugged, and listening devices had been placed in the heat registers and under the bed. Any direct conversations about the brothers between Gerd and Jo were written down, read, then flushed down the toilet.

Day six of the holiday was a free day. Gerd and Jo decided to shop and browse in the area of their potential contact. They could not go to the Pastor's apartment for security reasons. The only hope for a transfer was that somehow, with God's help, they would see this brother and carefully and discreetly transfer their high value package without detection. For sure, a friendly warm Christian greeting with embraces and salutations was not possible.

Gerd and Jo had never met their contact, but they had seen a photo of him earlier and had studied it carefully. By observing certain facial identifiers they would know they were dealing with the correct person. Those marks were three warts just above the left eyebrow—the center one orange-brown in color and the size of a dime. The other two were black and small. And Gerd was quite certain the man did not know they were coming. He had to hear it from God. In the dark days of Communism that is precisely what happened. Christians learned to hear the voice of God out of necessity.

Finally day seven arrived. Gerd and Jo were to fly back to Germany later that day. The airline called them to say there would be a five-hour delay, giving them another afternoon to look for their contact. This extra time seemed to be a gift from God.

Gerd decided to make one more attempt. This time he would go alone and leave Jo to pack. He chose to travel by subway and crisscross the downtown core of Moscow, riding the two trains that bordered closest to the contact's apartment. For some reason the streets and subway were extremely busy, and his "trailers" were following. But it is more difficult to keep track of a person when the subway is packed full. Gerd planned to take each train three times and if he could not connect then, he would take it that God wanted him to return home with his precious cargo.

God was with him. The agents trailing him had been squeezed slightly away from him by the crush of the crowd. They were in the same train car but now they were a few feet away. A large lady wearing a huge fur coat and a big hat blocked the vision between Gerd and his trailers. Miracle of miracles, on a midtown stop his contact entered his car and took the only available seat directly behind him. As he sat down, Gerd turned to look at his face. There it was! The orange mole with two black ones beside. This was the man. Eye contact was made but no words. The contact was carrying a shopping bag as is common in Moscow, and he propped the top open. At the bottom of the bag, Gerd could see the binding side of a Bible. This was the moment.

How to make the exchange? Gerd wore a long winter coat and it reached right to the top of the shopping bag.

Because the subway was jammed with people, everyone was swaying back and forth and trying to hold on to the grip handles. The final confirmation was four blinks of the right eye responded to by Gerd with two from his right eye. Gerd gently and discreetly withdrew one arm inside his coat, pulled up his shirt, and gave a quick jerk to the money packet to get it off his back.

At that moment, the subway train braked hard. The passengers lurched first in one direction, then the other. As everyone was trying to prevent himself or herself from falling, he dropped the money packet into the top of the bag. The brother quickly pulled the bag closed and exited the subway as the train came to a final stop. Transfer done!

No KGB followed the man off the train and Gerd's trailers were not able to see what happened. Two stops later Gerd also exited the subway with the police following him. He walked back to his hotel and headed for the airport with Jo.

Some weeks later, Westerners who were in Moscow were told that six of the ten brothers were already released from jail and the others would be out soon. God be praised!

Chapter 4

THE PLOT THAT SUCCEEDED

Author's note:

During the Communist years, the entire Soviet bloc of nations was closed to the open practice of religion. Strict laws banned religious assembly, the receiving of monies (i.e. offerings) was illegal under currency law, and Bibles were considered contraband. If Bibles were found in homes or vehicles, they were confiscated and the persons involved suffered many indignities from the authorities. Fines and jail were frequent penalties. Many noble brave people from the West traveled into Soviet bloc nations past strictly controlled border stations to deliver Bibles, often putting their lives and freedoms in jeopardy to help the oppressed church and its members. In response to the question "How did you survive?" the answer heard most often was prayer and the Bibles sent from the West. The following is one of those stories that occurred in a former Soviet bloc nation.

In a small, quaint town near the eastern border of Germany, a group of entrepreneurial believers had developed a humanitarian mission. That was its public reputation. The advertised goal was to send food, clothing, and medical help to oppressed church people in the East and, to a lesser degree, elsewhere. On the grounds of the mission was a home for the mission director and several barn-like buildings where clothing and goods were sorted and repacked for shipment.

To help fund the mission, a for-profit auto collision repair shop operated in one of the mission buildings. This shop provided business and revenue and something more—an off-limits area at the back of the automotive building. To gain entry into that area one had to pass through a double-locked door with iron grates, then another door, and past an armed guard. "Off limits" meant precisely that.

The auto repair workers had an excellent reputation for their work. There was a reason. They were all automotive engineers with extensive experience in auto design, model fabrication, and the making of metal parts. In the "off limits" area these men would renovate camper vans and cars and small trucks that looked like normal vehicles, but that could carry hundreds, and sometimes thousands, of Bible portions.

I personally observed one Volkswagen van on which the workers had invested $60,000 cash and three months in work to make it suitable for Bible transportation. In that vehicle, 4,000 New Testaments could be hidden. As you can well understand, these vehicles had high value and strategic capability.

Documents were produced as required for the countries through which the vehicle would pass. I observed one file in which there were twenty titles for one vehicle.

Most transport trips were made between May and September since during that period a trip with a small motor home or a van-camper looked very much like a holiday excursion many people took during those months. The goal was to look as normal as possible. Also, during those months the borders were clogged with vehicles. The guards were busy, so perhaps they would not look too closely. In reality, they would have to dismantle the vehicle to get to the Bibles if they did not know the location of the various switches and panels.

In mid-summer one year, a new van-camper had been prepared and loaded with New Testaments. The traveling team consisted of a German couple and another young lady with her small child. German is widely spoken in European Russia and the "drop" was to be made in an area where many locals spoke German. The team looked like friends going on a holiday.

The goal was to be at the border at 3 P.M. The guards changed shifts at that time, and hopefully the outgoing shift would be too tired to deal with more vehicles and the new shift would not be fully up to speed. However, no one could accurately predict the length of lines or the intensity of inspections at any crossing. There was always substantial risk. If even one Bible was found, problems escalated to an alarming stage.

After prayer for divine help, the team drove into the border crossing's "no man's land"—the zone where there is no going back and no going forward without inspection. There was no foliage. All trees had been cut, and fences were twelve feet high topped with razor sharp wire. Guards were posted in towers, and huge cement-filled pipes lay across the roadway to prevent anyone from crashing through into the next country. Electronic surveillance equipment was visible everywhere. Such border posts had been built to intimidate as well as process travelers.

Present at every border station was the dreaded KGB, the secret police, along with the normal customs and immigration personnel. In Romania this group was called *Securitate,* and in East Germany, the *Stasi.* They both spied on people and intimidated them. They were the hammer the Communist party used to beat the population into submission and fear.

The border crossing was very busy this day and a light rain was falling. The van finally pulled into an inspection point and all documents were presented. They were, of course, in perfect order. One wrong or overlooked item and transit would be forbidden. The purpose of the visit was to "visit around the villages, museums, and nearby seashore." They were asked to pull through and go into another inspection area. Not a good thing.

A customs officer came and looked through two bags of personal items and let them pass. They were *in!*

The map to the Bible drop point had been memorized. Obviously the risk of exposure would be high with any kind of written documents. There were no notes with addresses of people or any other contacts. Everything was "in mind" and nowhere else. Present in the van were regular roadmaps, travel brochures, and accommodation information. Everything about the vehicle made it look like a holiday was in progress and nothing else.

Most Westerners who crossed the border were followed. As a car went through a town, local police would record the time and direction of travel. In the next town the same, and so on. If the car did not arrive in the next town in a reasonable time, out came the police to find it. The Bible team rented a space by the sea for three days. They visited a nearby castle and made all the appearances of being on vacation. These acts tended to calm down the police and created a bit of space and time for other activities.

As the team traveled from place to place, they would stop in a shady place next to the road for a picnic style lunch. This is a common practice throughout Europe. It was another attempt by the team to look "normal" and not stand out. The Bible drop was to be near one of the forested areas in the countryside. Measured from the road one passed when leaving a nearby town, the Bibles were to be dropped precisely 6.1 kilometers further out and into a weeded ditch near the edge of the highway.

The drop was to take place on the eighth day of the teams' holiday. As they passed through the last town before the drop, they noticed the local police recording their direction of travel and the time. Quickly they saw the sign from which they were to measure the next 6.1 kilometers. They arrived at the spot and set up their picnic table under a large tree. Food was brought out and the young mother and her child sat to eat. Anton, the young man on the team acted like he was checking the vehicle, cleaning off bugs, and looking at the tires.

Inside the van, his wife was at work She was unscrewing two screws under the dashboard that, when loosened would allow the entire dash assembly and steering column to telescope into the back of the van. This movement of the panels exposed the Bibles. She quickly stuffed them into black trash bags. The process was repeated at the back of the van until all the Bibles were in black bags. The child was kept outside so he could not see what was happening.

The last Bibles had just been loaded and Anton had moved around to the front of the van when, to his great upset, a police car with two officers pulled up bumper to bumper with the van. At the same time, a farm truck came alongside the police car. The truck driver jumped out, went to the passenger side of the police car, and apparently started telling jokes. The police officers were laughing hysterically. The officer on the passenger side tried three times to open the door, but the truck driver pressed his ample belly against it and made them laugh again. (Keep in mind, the police were not more than four feet from the 4,000 Bibles in the back of the van.)

After a few minutes of tug-of-war and jokes, the police started their engine and backed away. The truck driver climbed back into his truck and motioned for Anton to come around to the opposite side. The driver handed him four pears, pointed towards heaven, and drove off. There were four on the team. Wonder how the driver knew that?

As soon as the highway was clear and everyone's heart rate was back to normal, Anton checked a little path across the road for the proper sign that this was, in fact, the drop point. It was. Hurriedly, thirty-five heavy bags were moved. In a few minutes, the Bibles were at their pickup point, hidden between two old-growth trees. The team's journey resumed to the border and the night was spent nearby in a camping site. The next day there were no problems crossing the border and returning home.

May I ask you, who was that truck driver? How did he know to give four pears to Anton? What was he saying to the police? Why did he point heavenward when he drove off?

I wonder.

Chapter 5

A PROPHET'S PREDICTION

Chickens, cows, people, and sheep all wander around the dusty streets of Schela (pronounced skay-lah), a small, poor village on the east side of Romania. Schela is all about farming. The people who live there are simple, big-hearted, and wonderfully hospitable. The village is near the Moldovan/Ukrainian/Romanian borders, an area that was deemed high security during the Communist years.

The leaders of the Old Russian Empire were driven and controlled by fear. They were fearful when there was nothing and no one to be afraid of. For instance, the city of Galati—located about twenty kilometers from Schela, with a population of approximately 400,000 inhabitants—is the only major city in Romania that does not have an airport. The Russians thought it was too near their borders. To have an airport in Galati was perceived in Moscow as a security risk; thus no airport was built there during the seventy-five years of Communist rule.

The people of Schela and other similar villages suffered heavy persecution simply because of their location. Due to the prevailing political mood of the Communist period, Schela was ruled by a heavy-handed, party-loyal Communist. The rigors of Communist rule were severe, and the hand of government was heavy upon everyone. The price for disobeying any rules, written or unwritten, was high.

The Communist "manager" (ruler of the area) constantly oppressed the small band of believers in Schela. Harassment, false arrests, police intimidation, imprisonment, and public humiliation were common. For many years the only meetings for Christians were held in homes, in small numbers, and quietly. Bible fragments were read, then re-read to sustain the hearts of the faithful. The discovery by the authorities of any religious literature resulted in jail.

One day a hearty person kindly offered a garden plot as a building site for a new church. Everyone knew there was no way permission would be granted for a church. Permission to build any church had to be issued in Bucharest, and that was not going to happen easily under Communist rule. If the Communists did not refuse—which they would— the Orthodox Church would reject the idea, because they also had to approve any church building plans anywhere in the country.

Believers in Schela went about their farming, many fasting and praying for wisdom from God. The first bit of help from the Lord came in the form of a person who prophesied in a house meeting that a very narrow window of opportunity was going to open in the future to build a house for God. How should the people prepare for that time? The prophet said that the people should begin slowly and discreetly to collect building materials. In farm districts it is common to have lumber and/or timbers around, as well as blocks, nails, and cement. Possession of these materials could easily be explained if necessary.

In the following months, the believers quietly followed the prophet's instructions and collected building materials of various kinds—a board here and a block there. Glass for window sash was stored in the hay barns.

Someone developed building plans for the small lot and for a building to fit it. During this time, the people kept pressing the "town manager" for permission to build a church. His response came in higher levels of anger. But the people were not discouraged by the rejections. They continued to pray and collect building materials.

After many months, the manager called the townspeople together to browbeat them again with Communist ideology. The goal was to weaken and intimidate them into following the party line. His ploy did not work. The people pressed all the more for permission to build a small church. In a state of explosive anger, the manager said, "I will give you the same deal as in the New Testament. You have three days. If you can build a church in three days I will permit it."

Little did the manager know that the people were *ready* to build. They had the plans, all the required materials, and the passion to build a house for God. In less than six hours the materials were at the site. Construction started immediately and continued twenty-four hours a day for three days and three nights.

At the end of the third day, a small chapel had been "roughed in" in Schela. The finish work and paint was still needed, but the exterior walls were up and the roof on.

On the third evening the manager returned. The believers knew he would be angry when he saw what they had done. However, he was struck with awe that a few Christians could build a church in three days. He thought he had laid out his challenge in such a way that no building would be possible. But it was! God was with the believers of Schela in a powerful way. After seeing what had been done, the manager left town in a rage but agreed that the believers could keep their church. He had to keep his word or risk a riot.

I have been blessed to have preached in the church at Schela. It is a genuine credit to the faith and persistence of the people of that village.

Chapter 6

DIVINE APPOINTMENTS

The Communist party enforcers, called the KGB or secret police, put heavy-handed pressure on the Christian community. Houses were invaded without warning; Bibles and Christian literature confiscated, and penalties levied in the form of money, jail time, lost employment, and public embarrassment. The children of Christians were not allowed in universities. In extreme cases, so-called "offenders" were sent to Siberia as punishment.

Every believer was especially sensitive as to the persons they spoke with and in whose company they were seen in public. No one wanted anyone else to be arrested or placed in a situation where they were endlessly questioned. Caution was the watchword that controlled socializing. The KGB treated everyone with suspicion.

One of the most persecuted brothers was Yoan. He had been born and raised in the capital city of his country. He had been successful in his career and after a few years had been appointed second in command of a government enterprise. One of Yoan's workers had been sharing his testimony and newfound faith with him. After some months, Yoan accepted Jesus Christ as his personal savior. His life changed so radically and so quickly his superiors hardly knew him as the same man. Very quickly the KGB learned of Yoan's religious inclinations and arrested him.

Yoan and his family were sentenced to exile inside their own country in a remote area far from the capital, their home, and friends. The house he was ordered to live in was at the end of a short road where all the trees had been cut down around it. The KGB wanted to be able to trace every movement. Because of faith in Christ, Yoan was demoted from his high executive position to a job running an elevator in a coal mine. The KGB also assigned him work shifts on Sunday to keep him from engaging in any church services or religious activities.

The government did everything they could to isolate Yoan. But a man of God is never alone or without influence. He immediately began to share his faith with his coworkers. In a few months, many had been born again and came to his house for fellowship and Bible study.

The severity of government persecution made it essential that all windows be closed and curtains drawn tight. Worship and prayers were whispered as the KGB had listening devices that could overhear conversations from a half-mile away. Anyone who came to Yoan's house for fellowship came at night, stayed a night or two, and departed again at night. Most did not use the nearby road, but chose to walk through the fields to escape detection. Times were hard for the church, but they still came!

Despite all they experienced, God continued to give Yoan favor with people. Often Catholic priests came to visit because their parishioners had changed lives and the priests wanted to know why. Many priests and nuns were saved in those days.

Visitors from the West were few. If foreigners were caught doing religious work, more pressure fell on the local believers. One time a group from the West wanted to visit. Yoan had no phone and all his mail was intercepted by the secret police, so if someone wanted to visit, they had to ask God about the timing of their trip. The Western leaders sensed the timing was right to go, so they headed into Yoan's country.

At an interim stop, they had hoped to meet with some other brothers on the edge of the capital city. They detoured slightly to go to that house meeting. En route they stopped for fuel. While fueling the car, one of the brothers felt strongly they should not go on to the prearranged meeting. This turned out to be a leading from God as the meeting was raided later that day and all the participants were arrested and endlessly questioned. The Westerners made haste to travel onward to the area where Yoan lived. They planned, like most others, to arrive at night.

Late that night they passed through the nearest town to Yoan's house. They thought it was strange that the police station in that town was closed and shuttered, but it was learned later that the local police officers were at a conference 100 miles away. On every road there was a police station and traffic checkpoint every few kilometers. One of these checkpoints was at the corner of the road leading to

Yoan's house. The Westerners quickly and quietly pulled into Yoan's barn.

After tapping on the house door with a pre-arranged code, the door opened; the Westerners entered, and were taken to the basement. All the basement windows had been painted black from the inside so anyone outside could not see any light.

Yoan was home. God had prompted him to go home from work. He also had been prompted to pray that twenty-two men he was training for leadership would come to his house. Twenty were already there and the other two arrived shortly thereafter. Yoan told his Western visitors he had been praying for someone to come and teach about Jesus and His Word. They were an answer to prayer.

How did the twenty-two men know to come? They had been prompted in their spirit by prayer. Hearing the Father's voice for guidance was the way the underground church operated. There was no other way to receive information because all means of communication were strictly controlled by the government and the secret police. There are multitudes of testimonies of God's faithfulness in speaking to His people directly and specifically.

For the next six hours the teaching went on nonstop with brief breaks only for coffee or soup. The brothers were starving for teaching from God's Word. After listening to the teaching the second night till almost dawn, the brothers began to slip out, but not more than two at a time. Fortunately the night was cloudy and overcast. The morning light had begun to shine when the last of the guests, the Westerners, thought it was time to go.

42

As they went to the barn to retrieve their car, they heard the sound of a small airplane nearby. There are almost no small planes in that area even today, so it was a noticeable sound during those Communist years. One brother had started the car and backed it out so all the rest could load. The plane had dropped down to less than 300 feet in altitude and was flying directly overhead.

It then turned around and began to slowly fly back and forth over Yoan's house.

One of the brothers noticed a long-range lens sticking out of one window. This intruder was obviously a government plane and a KGB agent was taking photos. By this time everyone had already had more than one picture taken.

Standing near the barn were Yoan and his wife and the Westerners. They prayed for one another and for protection for all. One brother said, "Yoan, is there anything you would like us to tell the brothers in the West?" He said, "Yes, there are two things I would like to say. First, ask them to pray for us because, as you can see, we have a few problems. Second, tell the brothers that Jesus said, 'I will build my church and the gates of hell will not prevail against it.'" Everyone said a loud Amen!

The car was searched carefully to be sure there were no Bibles, religious literature, or anything else that would connect the Westerners to Yoan and his family. With the check complete, the team headed for the border hoping for an easy crossing.

The crossing ultimately took six hours as the entire team was strip-searched. Everything was taken out of the suitcases, and the car seat removed. One Country and Western music cassette was found and listened to in its entirety before the team was released.

Yoan became a major leader in the underground church. Within a few months of his internal exile, more than 150 leaders would sneak into his home at night. All the weekends were used for training and prayer, even though Yoan had to work from 4 A.M. till noon. Other people would teach during those hours. In Yoan's mind, training and teaching were paramount.

When the Westerners asked Yoan about his primary need, he answered, "We need teaching more than anything." He then asked, "Could you come back and teach for several days?" The team responded that they would be happy to return, but they questioned how such an event could be organized in such pressure-filled conditions.

Yoan's response shocked the brothers. He said that local brothers would arrange five potential spots for training locations, all of which were in the woods. The local brothers would then pray and God would tell them where to meet and they would be guided to the proper spot. One of the western brothers said he needed to know specifically where he was going to be at all times so his family could stay in touch.

Yoan answered in a way that displayed his faith: "Just ask the Father and you will arrive where we are. We trust Him to guide you to us." The Westerners stood wide-eyed in disbelief. Though they walked with God at a certain faith level, it clearly was not the same as the brothers in this country. There were no phones or faxes. Even if they had been available, they would have been electronically bugged.

So, the brothers turned to God in faith believing and God did not disappoint them.

With that in their spirit and ears, the Westerners departed for their own country.

Chapter 7

A VISITOR SENT FROM GOD

Author's note:

Slowly, carefully, and discerning were the guide words for sharing the gospel in the Communist days. It was slow and dangerous work. One could not be too careful. Even your best friend could be a secret informant for the KGB. And if not a regular informer, almost everyone could be intimidated by a late night visit from the secret police with guns drawn. This means of extracting information usually worked because the next level was beatings, jail, or a Siberian train trip in winter.

Vlad had been raised in a small, poor village near a large industrial city. The house he lived in was a patchwork of different sorts of boards, some sheets of metal, some plastic sheeting, and doors made from rough-cut lumber. Floors were not solid. The outside of the house was covered with black tarpaper. All the houses in the villages looked like this. The toilet was outside in summer, and a "honey bucket" was used in winter. The family was poor but had a sense of grand dignity about them. They had hope!

Vlad's home place always had a small assortment of animals—the most important being the pigs and the cow that provided milk and meat. In summer, a large garden produced table vegetables and a good supply of potatoes and cabbage for winter. But for three years the summers had been rainy, cloudy, and cold. There were no food supplies remaining.

To buy food for his two children and wife, one day Vlad went to the city in search of a job. Earlier his father had located an old machine, rebuilt it from parts or made parts, and turned out a few products to sell for extra money. From his dad Vlad had learned how to use machine tools, so he didn't think he would have trouble finding work. For several days he went from factory to factory. On the third day he was offered a position and soon began working as an apprentice to a toolmaker.

From time to time Vlad would help his father at home. One day, a man came with a local Communist leader and wanted some truck parts made for the military. The government was the only business in existence. Thus, that was the entity with which one had to do business. Because the tools and machines in Vlad's shop were not adequate for the task before them, a good used machine was offered if Vlad and his father would agree to do the work needed.

In due season the machine arrived, along with an inventory of metals for parts. For three years everything went well. With the extra earnings, the house was repaired and made more livable. The work shed was further insulated from the cold. With the increasing orders, Vlad and his father hired several more people. Soon Vlad owned a nice car, took his family to the Black Sea for holidays, and one summer even traveled to Western Europe. Those perks were precious indeed under the Communist regime.

In the fourth year of operations, tragedy struck twice. Vlad's mother died within two weeks of being diagnosed with cancer. Six months later his father died from a heart attack and asthma. Vlad went into a deep depression.

He was now alone in the house and alone in running the business. But with his skills, the business continued to grow. He was able to get production out in a timely way (almost unheard of in those days) and with good quality (also a rarity). He soon built a building to expand the business, one adequate for more machines and inventory.

Because he had money, his fair-weather friends were many. He liked wine and a glass of vodka at the end of the workday. Whatever the time, when his friends came around, the drinking began. It kept increasing until alcohol was a growing problem in Vlad's life.

Soon Vlad's family relationships became strained. His sons were being neglected, and the business began to taper off because of the decrease in quality and production time. He also lost several long-term employees because of his volatile temper and outbursts. The days were becoming darker.

After several warnings from his buyers in the government, a message came that a highly-placed official was coming to visit. Vlad was struck with fear as this visitor had the power to terminate his contracts and remove some of the machines that had been loaned to him by the government. And Vlad did not know this man. The other managers below him were friends, but not this man. He was the top official in the entire region.

To Vlad's surprise, the official seemed to be an entirely different kind of person from the others who had come previously. He did not smoke or curse, nor did he drink alcohol. He refused the standard vodka party at day's end. Though very businesslike, he also manifested a special warmth Vlad did not understand.

What kind of a man was this? He was unlike anyone else who had been sent from the government. He was strict and authoritarian, but not abusive, and he did not generate fear. He spoke kindly with all the workers and accepted an invitation for a meal in Vlad's home. While there, Vlad's sons treated him like a playmate and he acted like a newfound uncle. Compliments were also paid to Myrna, Vlad's highly-intimidated wife. Vlad had several shots of vodka as he offered toast after toast, but the officer just had water every time. "Nyet" was his standard answer to alcohol.

After the boys and Myrna had gone to bed, Vlad and the official talked long into the night. Finally, the officer said to Vlad, "Have you ever thought about God? We have been taught there is no God, but what if—just what if—the people who said that were wrong?"

Vlad answered that he had wondered from time to time what kept the old village women going to the Orthodox Church down the road. He had been there a time or two and felt out of place. He did not understand the language and all the symbols.

"No," the officer said, "I don't mean the church building and all that. I mean could there be a real God somewhere? Are those old ladies looking for Him? Have they found Him?"

Vlad could not answer such a question. It did stir his thinking, but it was dangerous to be thinking about God. He was officially nonexistent.

The official put Vlad and his factory on probation. Work and production had to improve in ninety days or their work would be given to others. Three months later, the official returned with other government inspectors. Because of Vlad's discipline, his work and production numbers had improved significantly and the inspectors were pleased. Afterward the official offered a reciprocal meal at his home in another city. Relieved from the potential of termination and bankruptcy, Vlad gladly accepted.

The meal was served in multiple courses. The evening went by quickly. Soon Vlad and the official were alone in front of a warm wood fireplace. In this setting the officer shared his personal journey from military school all the way to his current high position. His early years had been filled with partying, drunkenness, and drug use. Alcohol had controlled his life. One night on a training exercise, a young recruit said, "If this was really war and we all died, would we meet God?" He could not answer because that question went to the core of his thoughts.

Without speaking again for more than an hour, the recruit heard a story from his commander. It started in childhood with exposure to Communist ideology. Later came training in Kosomol, the Communist youth organization, then on to a career in the military. Finally someone secretly handed him a Bible. With that gift, everything began to change in his life. His friend who gave it simply asked him to read it and then report his thoughts. In his reading and search, Jesus Christ became real to him. The commander then told Vlad he had a capacity for God that was huge. He reached beneath his seat and handed Vlad a Bible and, like someone had done to him, simply asked him to read it. "See if you can find God in there," was his instruction.

Vlad traveled back home with the Bible hidden in his work orders. After another round of binge drinking and partying, he saw his true condition and realized he could not change himself. Night after night he read the Bible. As happened to his friend the official, the Bible began to speak to his heart's condition. On the last page of the Bible was a prayer written so seekers could ask Christ into their hearts. After praying it the third time, Vlad began to weep and could not stop for most of the night. He knew something had happened but was not sure what. He did not know any Christians (in the born-again sense). One major change came immediately. The next time vodka was offered, it became sour in his mouth. He spit it out and did not touch it again.

The weeks passed and both family and workers noticed the changes in his Vlad's life. He did not understand what was happening, but things were radically different in a good way. Some former employees came back to see what this new man was like. His current employees went on with their lives and all the problems attached to them.

Because of political sensitivities, Vlad did not utter a word about God or his Bible.

That was just too dangerous. As noted earlier, anyone—including your closest friend—could be a government shill passing information to the secret police. Vlad's wife had become a believer as well. One by one his employees would ask him about the changes in his life and most of them became followers of Jesus. In a little more than a year, all his employees had accepted Christ as Savior. Because there was just one Bible, they had to copy a page at a time to have Scripture for all to read.

For the next five years, Vlad did not meet another Christian except the official from the government and his workers. He saw this official once a year, and nothing about God could be discussed via phone or letters since both were monitored. But he kept reading the Bible day by day. More and more love for Jesus grew in him. His workers openly discussed questions about the Bible and God inside the shop.

Vlad decided some answers might be forthcoming if they studied together. With the possibility of arrest by the KGB and the threat of business and personal liberties lost, he offered to have a Bible study in his home on Sunday mornings twice a month. The plan was to turn on the machines to mimic production sounds, but all the workers would be in the house studying the Bible.

Miracles still happen today. On one Sunday morning when the Bible study was about to start, a man from Ghana appeared at the door and announced God had sent him. How could this be? God sent someone all the way from Africa to a small Russian village, and a Christian at that. Did God really speak to people as clearly as this? The man spoke Russian as he had been trained as an engineer in Russia.

The Ghanaian had flown to the large industrial city nearby, took a taxi to the center of town, and had then walked following the directions he said the Lord gave him in a dream. He said he had come to preach the gospel from the Bible. Vlad's group was both stricken with fear of discovery on the one hand and blessed beyond expression on the other. What to do? They decided this whole event must be the Lord's doing, so they allowed the brother to proceed.

A black man with bags in his hand walking through a Russian village on Sunday morning does attract attention. Walking and visiting was one thing, but preaching from the Bible was a forbidden and punishable offense. Sure enough, after just a few minutes of preaching, a platoon of soldiers arrived at the door of the house and demanded that the preacher be brought out.

Great boldness came over Vlad. He responded to the military leaders by saying "No, he will not come out. It is rude behavior and bad manners to interrupt someone when they are speaking, so he will not come out."

The military leader was struck with almost childlike tenderness. He replied, "You are correct. We will wait in the trucks until he is finished."

More than an hour passed, and because the soldiers did not hear preaching, they came again to arrest the guest and probably Vlad as well. Again the military police demanded that the Ghanaian come out of the house.

Vlad said, "No. He cannot come out. He is too tired from preaching and is resting, so he cannot come out." Again the officer acted as though he were a child and said, "We will wait near our trucks until your guest has rested."

After two hours more, the platoon leader came to the door for the Ghanaian. Vlad again said, "No, he cannot come out. He is hungry from preaching and now must eat, so he cannot come out."

Finally the leader said, "You are right. We want our guests to be treated well here." With that he gave a signal and the platoon drove off, not to be seen again.

Throughout the afternoon and evening the Ghanaian brother greatly encouraged Vlad's little group. He predicted the fall of communism within three years and encouraged them to be bold in their faith because, as they had seen that day with the military police being humbled like children, God was with them. The gospel was going to be preached no matter how much opposition Communist governments practiced.

The visitor answered questions until eleven o'clock that evening. Love was expressed for them all and he departed, saying he was on a holy assignment to another place. To get there safely, he had to cross a border at a specific time when guards were dozing. Into the dark he went—a visitor sent from God.

Chapter 8

SOLITARY SENTINEL

Author's note:

Like in other stories in this book, we thought it prudent not to use the actual names of people and places. Why? Some who count Jesus as Savior are working in security-sensitive areas. Through the sharing of these stories we want to encourage faith and hope. At the same time, we do not want to jeopardize the personal safety or work of any fellow believer. Increasingly, Christians are being pressured now, by the government and traditional religious leaders.

Travel with me in your mind to the frozen north of the Russian republic and to the arctic prison camps located there. In one location accessible only by train, there were twenty-three prison encampments. No one has ever been known to escape them—ever! At the height of the Communist years dozens of these prison camps were in existence.

Both political dissenters and religious protestors were confined with segregation. The nearest estimate I have found concerning the number of believers who were incarcerated and ultimately died exceeds five million persons during the Stalin years alone. Millions died from disease and mistreatment, and some were cremated.

There were no roads to the prison camps, only one rail spur on which both supplies and prisoners were transferred from a town sixty kilometers away. The only way into that town was by rail, and it was five hundred kilometers from any city of reasonable size. The train went back and forth once a week. There was no airport within hundreds of kilometers and no roads close by either. If a prisoner did escape the physical confines of the camp, how would he get out of the area? Especially in winter, death from freezing would come within a few short hours.

For the "crime" of sharing the gospel with his family, friends, a nephew, and a few work mates, a young brother was arrested at night, tried before a corrupt tribunal, and sent to one of the prison compounds mentioned above. This means of arrest at night was called the "midnight call" and was greatly feared by the people in general as most persons taken away by this means were never heard from again. When the boys protested, they were sarcastically advised to "get help from your Christian friends."

We shall call this young man Ivan. He was put into solitary confinement and was kept from all medical care for the first five years of his imprisonment. He was also assigned to a "hard labor" group for several years of what would eventually be a twenty-four year imprisonment.

Fortunately, because of God's sustaining strength and the kindness of a few other prisoners, Ivan was able to manage, even though he suffered a great deal physically. Prison conditions were fit more for animals than humans. Toilets were holes cut in a concrete slab. They often had to be shoveled out because the prison camp was on the Tundra and there was no disbursement of liquids into the soil. Everything underground was frozen. It was usually the "religious" prisoners who were given the nasty duty of shoveling the pile of excrement.

Living quarters were crowded; the sick, insane, and well prisoners all living together and trying to survive. Food was like gruel; its poor nutritional value was one of the reasons so many prisoners were sick. Any cold or flu-type disease spread quickly to most prisoners. Sleeping was fitful at best and not possible at worst. Some prisoners walked around all night, some screamed. In the midst of that noise and confusion, others tried to sleep. In winter, staying warm was the challenge. In summer, flies came across the Siberian plains and stung people mercilessly.

That, dear reader, is the environment to which a man of God was sent. Was it because he was evil and sinful? No. He was in prison for sharing the gospel. By any civilized standard, the situation was inhumane, cruel and unfair—but needful.

Ivan gained great favor with his fellow prisoners. He was kind, willing to listen, and shared his faith with all who would dare to hear his witness. He openly prayed for those who asked. At every opportunity he shared Christ with inmates and guards alike. His reputation spread to other camps in the area through the guards and workers, and many quietly sought his advice and counsel. Prisoners were often rotated from prison to prison to keep them from developing friendships. Because of this rotation system, Ivan was able to meet many prisoners and tell them of his faith in Jesus. These interactions and the hope released from them were a fulfilling ministry by itself. But there was much more.

After seven years of confinement, and in the midst of an extremely cold and difficult winter, something unusual started to happen that continued on and off for the next several years. Usually when Ivan was transferred between camps, he was placed in solitary confinement for a few months due to the fact that he continued to share Jesus with anyone who would listen. In the horrible despair of the prison camps, he had a message of hope and was, therefore, considered dangerous. What the Russian prison planned for evil, however, God began to turn to good. Something truly amazing started to happen.

During a particularly noisy night punctuated by sounds of some being beaten, others screaming from nightmares, and the fiendish laugh of the mentally unstable, Ivan heard his cell door rattle. It was gentle, but it was the sound usually made when someone was entering. Ivan's eyes had been open a long while anyway because of the noise and they had long since adjusted to the darkness. The moonlight coming through his narrow window allowed him to see all the way across his cell. He heard the door rattle two more times and then it was quiet.

More than an hour passed. For the third time, there was a gentle rattle followed by the unmistakable sound of his cell door opening. Yet Ivan could see no one and the door did not seem to move. At this middle-of-the-night moment, the guards were all at a central station either asleep or eating. They were not concerned with the status of the prisoners who were unable to escape.

Upon hearing another rattle and click, Ivan tried his door. To his amazement, the lock had been reset and, although the door was closed, the locking mechanism had been unlocked. The door was open! It did not unlock like this every night, but it did unlock three to five times per week for the next several years.

Ivan did not try to leave his cell at first, thinking this could be a trick and would result in even more severe punishment and perhaps death. But soon he began to realize why he was in solitary. Prisoners would come and go through this part of the prison. They came to be "broken," which meant tortured and beaten. Many died. But at night, when the guards were away and his cell rattled, he knew it was time to go from cell to cell talking quietly and praying with those who would listen. Speaking in whispers and hushed tones, he led hundreds of men to Christ during his time in solitary confinement.

Ivan also recorded the times of the guard patrols. He would slip back into his cell and wait for them to pass. When they shook his door, it always seemed to be locked, but as soon as they passed by it would rattle again gently and be unlocked.

An update;

In the late 1980s, Ivan was released from prison. By that time, thousands of men had been won to Christ. The days of "glasnost" (openness) came to Russia, and holding religious prisoners was no longer beneficial in the light of international relations.

At this writing, Ivan has some family members working as missionaries in the same camps where he was imprisoned. His former warden is now a Christian and a deacon in one of the churches that now operates freely in the prison camps.

Some of God's people are called upon to pay a high and heavy price in their service for Christ. Ivan was such a one. The Communist system confined his body but not his spirit or ministry. He won!

PART TWO:

Miracles in Asia

Chapter 9

MINISTER OF MIRACLES IN INDIA

Brother Abraham was born and raised in a densely forested area of India. Most Indian men do not live beyond their seventies, but when I met Abraham he was ninety-three years old. In spite of his age, if you were scanning a crowd you would notice him. He is a mighty man of God and has energy and dynamism bigger than life itself.

Abraham and I connected at a conference in the central part of India. In the first service I noticed him because he stood next to the aisle, carried a walking stick and a small cotton bag over his shoulder. I found out later that all his earthly possessions were in that little bag. He wore "Ben Franklin" type glasses that were always perched on the end of his nose. Two white shocks of hair stood straight up on his otherwise bald head. There he was—a man of God with beautiful brown skin wrapped in a white cotton garment.

Brother Abraham was noticeable for reasons beyond his appearance. He was a passionate participant in worship. In our first service at the conference, he stepped into the aisle, positioned his walking stick in front of him, and swayed back and forth as we sang. He worshiped with his face aglow and always tipped heavenward.

The coordinator of the conference saw me looking at Abraham and said, "Please remind me to tell you about him a little later." After the service, over coffee, I was told that "Old A" was one of the best church planters in India. "He prays till the name of a town, city, or village comes on his heart," the coordinator said. "Usually, those who want to become pastors go out with him to help plant and establish a church.

"Abraham begins with a miracle service," he continued. "Depending on the size of town or city, he will assemble a team to go house-to-house announcing a time of prayer for all the sick a few days hence. For instance, a team member may say, 'On Friday, a man of God will be in the city and he will pray for all sick people at noon in the center of the city. Bring all the blind, all the deaf, cripples, and even dead people.'

"Needless to say, crowds come from everywhere to see what God will do. Hundreds and sometimes thousands of people come in every condition imaginable. They have no other hope. They have no money or access to proper medical help. After Abraham prays, there is a short delay of silence. Then, suddenly people begin to scream, 'I can hear!' 'I can see!' and so forth. Testimonies are given publicly, and then the gospel is preached. Within a few days there are enough new believers to start a church."

Old Abraham is a "sent man" on a distinct mission to build the kingdom of God. His earthly goods are contained in a little cotton bag carried on his shoulder. His walking stick and Bible are his only other possessions. But what he lacks in material goods, he makes up for in power, anointing, and strength.

I was a personal witness to some special touches from God through this seasoned elder. For instance, one night I was leading the meeting and decided to personally pray for all the ministers. Since there were about 1,500 of them, we decided to pray for half one night and the other half the next. The evening meetings were open to the public, so those crowds were bigger.

The first night, half the leaders were called to the front for ministry and prayer. Abraham started down the center aisle with many others. When he arrived at the front, he was centered in the crowd left to right and near center back to front. And he was out in front of the podium about twenty feet. A good place to be for ministry. I knew hours and hours of ministry were ahead of us and help would be needed. Who better than Old A?

Speaking to him over the public address system so he could hear, I simply asked him to pray for the people around him and to release the presence of God into their lives. I was not ready for what happened. He did not lay hands on anyone or pray for anyone that I could see. He simply raised his hands heavenward and shouted "Jesus" a few times. With that utterance something from heaven came upon the leaders. Everyone within thirty feet of Abraham immediately fell over in God's presence. In the days following, many testified to significant encounters with the Lord that night.

A day or two later, something equally as wonderful occurred. In the midst of a morning teaching time, I felt led to minister to a young pastor who was severely depressed. Our platform was made up of two forty-foot flatbed trucks linked together for a total length of eighty feet. The podium was in the center, and this young pastor was seated on one end of the platform just gazing down at his feet.

I called Old A to help me because there were several others who were severely troubled in one way or another. When he arrived at the podium, I placed my arm around him so I could speak to him quietly about this troubled young pastor. From where Old A and I were standing, this young man was about forty feet away, and we were both looking at him.

Directly behind us, at the opposite end of the platform, two ministers were struggling to bring a demon-possessed lady onto the stage. Physically she acted like one who had an extreme case of cerebral palsy. Many doctors had reviewed her situation and could find nothing wrong with her. She and her family had been told they would just have to live with the situation. Some of her friends had brought her several hundred miles by train to be prayed for and delivered. It took two strong men to hold her upright.

Remember, Old A and I were looking in the other direction and we had our backs to her and her helpers. As I was instructing Old A on what I thought should be done with the depressed pastor, he gently raised his leathery hand and said, "Excuse me one moment, brother." He quickly whirled around to gaze at the young, possessed woman who was trembling and shaking. He lowered his raised hand and thrust it forward with his index finger pointing straight at the young woman. He did not utter a word. A great scream came out of the woman as the demons were expelled. She fell backward, was immediately delivered, stopped shaking, and her faculties were restored.

As Old A turned back towards me, he said, "Excuse me brother, I do not like the devil." With that, all his attention was now back on the young pastor, who was ministered to and received a great release in his life and mind.

My life has been deeply touched by Old Abraham. There are few like him. Oh God, may their tribe increase!

Chapter 10

AMBASSADOR EXTRAORDINAIRE

Author's note:

Traveling the world positions one in such a way that God can bring many others into the sphere of ministry. Personally, I count these encounters as "God moments" arranged for everyone's benefit. One such encounter, unplanned by me and seemingly incidental, happened in India. The encounter was with a church planter from another country in the area.

The Jeep with its young driver was making its way through congested traffic to take me to an appointment. In India, drivers are almost a necessity if one wishes to successfully navigate between vehicles of varying sizes and kinds, bicycles by the thousands, people walking in every direction in all lanes of traffic, and miscellaneous animals here and there. The smells wafting through the air further distract you—smells of spices, herbs, burning buffalo dung, human excrement, and pollution of every kind in large quantities. These are the sights and smells of India. It is a fascinating country.

In the midst of the traffic crawl, my driver became excited and pointed to a man walking ahead of our Jeep in the center of the street. The driver became even more animated and yelled, "Uncle, you must speak with this man. He is a man of God." (To protect this man and the place where he works, the names of both shall remain undisclosed. We will call him Thomas John-TJ if you will.) With that, he slammed the Jeep to a stop, jumped out and embraced the walking brother who was now directly in front of our vehicle. I hesitantly joined them. Introductions were made and I invited my new friend for tea.

TJ was raised in a nominal Hindu family. A friend had invited him to a home-based Bible study when he was fifteen. From that time on he couldn't get enough information to satisfy his interests. Through the class he began to hear about Jesus Christ. After some months, he accepted Jesus as his personal Savior. He took some literature home, and eventually his entire family accepted Christ and began attending a small Pentecostal church that met in a house.

During these years a genuine revival visited TJ's church. During the visitation of the Lord, TJ felt a call to full-time ministry. He sensed that he was specifically being sent by the Lord to a country that was, and is now, officially closed to gospel ministry of any kind. But the truth is no country is absolutely closed to God. One must be creative when thinking about methods.

TJ set himself to fasting and prayer for forty days, asking for wisdom from God about his assigned land. From

that special season of prayer, he felt he should set an appointment with the country's governor—the person who
handles the day-to-day business for the rulers.

No access was permitted. This highest level of the national administration claimed to be far too busy to give time
to a foreigner who had come to the country to preach a
foreign religion. Furthermore, TJ was sternly warned not
to preach publicly or privately.

TJ was rebuffed but not discouraged. He rented a small
room in a guesthouse and prayed day and night for two
weeks about what to do next. He knew God had sent him,
but he needed God's direction to know how to proceed.

In prayer, TJ sensed he should return to the governor's
office and to his appointment secretary. There he announced
he was an "ambassador." The appointment secretary did
not ask him what country he represented but went immediately to the governor's office and said, "There is an ambassador here to see you." With that introduction, TJ was
ushered into the governor's office.

Introductions were made and then the governor asked
a pertinent question, "Which country do you represent?
From which nation are you bringing credentials?"

TJ straightened his back and said, "I am an ambassador
for Jesus Christ. I represent the kingdom of God and His
Son, Jesus Christ."

The governor stood in anger and said, "You gained en-
trance here under false pretenses. You cannot preach any
religion in this country. If you do you will be killed or imprisoned."

TJ immediately responded, "Please sir, kill me and do it
quickly. If you kill me I shall be in an instant in the pres-

ence of my King. Thank you for wanting to kill me. Shoot me in the head so I can quickly meet my Lord. It will be an honor to die for Him."

"You must be crazy," the governor yelled. "I will not kill you and give you the honor and ease of sudden death. No. I will have you imprisoned for the rest of your life."

TJ responded again in the same manner as above. "Thank you, sir." With his hands crossed at the wrists he said, "Please take me now. In prison I could preach every day to all the prisoners about the goodness of Jesus and about how He can change their lives. Oh please sir, have me put directly in prison."

The governor said, "You have lost your mind. I want you to go out from here. I grant permission for you to stay in our country. You may also preach, but be quiet about it."

So TJ went out and began ministering. Cultural values in his country require families to provide bed and board to visitors for up to three days minimum without asking their names. So from village to village and town to town TJ went, preaching from house to house.

In five years time, thirty-six new churches had been planted through TJ's ministry, each with several families in membership. And this in a country that yet today is not open to public churches or missionaries. How then, is the above possible? There is a God in heaven who loves people. If we will follow Him, He will reveal creative ways for the gospel to be communicated.

An update. Last year the net number of house churches in the country where TJ works grew one hundred percent. God be praised!

Chapter 11

EVERY TRIBE
SHALL HEAR

Author's note:

A few years ago, there were a few tribes of people in the Philippines that were either unreached or under-reached. Some could be accurately described as being remote and primitive. A courageous missionary from Australia was burdened for those tribes and, in particular, a tribe called Matik Salig (pronounced Ma-teek Saw-lug). Following is the story of how they were initially touched.

During a high-level luncheon gathering of political and military leaders, missionary John was making his heart known to anyone who would listen who perhaps had access to the Matik Salig people. Who knew something about them? Was there a way to reach them or visit there? Where could he find someone to give him accurate information about that tribe?

Every report he had received about this tribe had been negative. They were headhunters who killed all trespassers in their tribal lands. They constantly carried out hostilities against other tribes around them. They were known to be extremely brave in battle, proprietary about their lands, and were animists religiously. No mission group had ever penetrated the area successfully with the gospel.

At the above mentioned luncheon, a blind lady listened to John as he spoke to a high level military leader. The leader warned him about even trying to make an attempt to travel in Matik territory. "It will cost you your life," he said, then related several stories of how people had suffered serious consequences when they tried to break into Matik territory. After these warnings, John walked away. But the blind lady called to him and asked him to sit down. She had some things to tell him.

"I know how to reach the Matik Salig," she said. "I will help you."

"How can you help me?" John asked.

"I know how to reach the Matik Salig people, the lady replied. Be prepared to travel in a few days."

Several days later, the blind lady and the missionary traveled to the island of Mindanao to arrange passage into the territory of the Matik Salig. A riverboat trip was arranged. After many hours on the river, the boat stopped just before a sweeping curve on the river. The riverboat was tied to a pier and the blind lady and their hired guide said, "This is as far we can go. Around the bend is the land of the Matik Salig and we cannot go any farther."

They located a translator who was willing to go for a fee, as well as a boat operator who knew that the Matik Salig traded in a nearby village around the bend in the river. So he was willing to go that far, but not further. After purchasing some supplies, they went to the villages of the Matik people.

The missionary and his attendants stopped at the first village and were received without threat. They told the locals what they wanted to do and set off in the direction of the highest mountains to find the Datu, or headman of the village at the top. After walking many hours, they came to a fork in the road and the boat operator said, "This is as far as I can go." With only a translator and no guides, John started through the jungle to the mountaintop.

When they arrived in a Matik village on the top of the mountain, there was no one in the village. The people had heard the outsiders coming up the trails and had gone into the jungle to hide until they felt safe. White men did not come to their villages. They had never seen one before.

John and his translator sat down in the center of the village and waited. Tribal custom was to wait for the Datu. When he was ready to speak with you or receive you, he would appear. After two or three hours of sitting alone and quiet, the Datu appeared. He squatted and for a period of several minutes said nothing. Then he spoke.

The Datu's first words were, "Why are the gods causing all our children to die?" The conversation opened and John and his friend explained why they had come. They then inquired concerning the condition of the children.

The Datu explained that the children were getting some spots on them, they got "hot" and then sicker and many died. John and the translator observed some of the children who were sick. The problem? Measles! The Matik had no natural immunity against this easily treated disease.

Without doctors and medical personnel nearby, the measles were taking the lives of dozens of young children.

John said, "I will help. I will go down the mountain and get medicine to help the children." He then trekked his entire journey in reverse to get to the city of Davao where he soon discovered that the medicines he needed in the quantity required would cost $77,000.

John didn't have that much money or the ability to get it quickly. He called the blind lady and she said, "This is not a problem. We will have the medicine soon from a source I have in the government." In a few days the medicine was available in Davao and ready to be transported to the Matik Salig mountain dwellers.

The arduous journey was repeated, going down the river, getting another boat and translator, then up the mountain many hours in rain forest conditions. Finally they arrived in the village of the Matik Salig, organized a vaccination program, and began inoculating the children. They immediately started getting better and the dying stopped.

Because of the medicine and kindness shown, John was able to preach the gospel to the Matik Salig, and dozens of them came to Christ. Today there is a viable church among the Salig tribes and the work of Christ continues to grow.

I am in mind of the Scripture that says, "every nation, tongue and tribe shall hear" (Revelation 14:6). Even the remote mountain tribal people of the Philippines shall hear. God be praised!

PART THREE:

Miracles in Latin America

Chapter 12

RESURRECTION POWER IN PERU

The South American nation of Peru has a backbone, the Andes Mountains, among the most difficult in the world to travel through. The roads are narrow and often impassible from washouts and lack of maintenance. Many are one lane requiring that if another vehicle comes from the opposite direction, some negotiating must be done to see who will back up, and how far, to find a space wide enough for two vehicles to pass. Those at the higher elevations have snow on them even through the summer months.

Travelers have three options. One is to walk. The second and most popular is to go by school-bus-type vehicles that have been specifically fitted for high elevation travel on treacherous roads. There are many of these vehicles; one can see them in every village with goods tied to the roof. And third, in certain places there is a narrow gauge British-built train. In its first four hours of travel out of the capital city of Lima, it passes through sixty tunnels ascending the Andes.

The people populating the Andes are called Quechuas. There are also many Spanish-Indian mixed races that are very poor. Many are illiterate. Most practice subsistence farming to provide food for their families. A major crop raised for cash is the coca plant from which the popular drug cocaine is derived.

Some larger towns serve as trade centers for surrounding villages. Typically there is a market day when everyone who wants to or needs to comes to town. There is some business and lots of drinking and partying. Most children have the opportunity for some schooling, but many are needed on the farms and do not attend. Few graduate. Overall, the high Andean plateaus are marked by all the classic Third World conditions.

A ministry teammate and I had lunch in the home of a believer in one of those high mountain towns. In that home I heard the following story. Interestingly, the people to whom these events happened were the ones who told me the story. An American missionary from the area confirmed the incident.

The home where we were having lunch was simple. There were no glass windows. The window openings were covered by shutters that were opened in the daytime. They were shut at night and in the later afternoon when it rained for about thirty minutes every day. The floors were finished roughly with cement in two rooms and wooden planks elsewhere. The toilet was outside, and there was no running water. Near the house was a well that served as the water source for the family.

The homeowner was a tradesman who made furniture in a large shed next to the house. The lady of the house was eight months pregnant with her seventh child, so she was busy tending to children and the house.

Our hosts were seated around a table. They included the pastor and two men from a local church. We Americans numbered three. Also, a young Quechua couple with an infant child and the aged mother of the young man were present. This family had been invited to visit with us because of a miracle that had occurred in their lives.

Rosa, the old Indian woman, had a face that glowed like the morning sun. She was dressed in local style, wearing between four to six skirts and as many blouses. The weather in the mountains could be very warm in the day and drop fifty degrees, sometimes more, at night. I suppose Rosa's clothing style could be called "early layering". Layers of clothing were added or taken off depending on the temperature. All the local people in the room knew Rosa, and they all had stories about "God moments" that happened through her prayers and life.

Rosa was constantly being called from one place or another to pray for people. Rich and poor, government and military leaders, even lepers—all had asked for Rosa's prayers at some time. The day prior to our visit she had been asked to pray for a terminally ill high-ranking military officer, and he had been instantly healed.

We were to hear an even greater miracle that had happened to her son who was present with us at lunch. Rosa had been away from her home village visiting and ministering to people. In her absence, her son had contracted a serious illness, accompanied by a dangerously high fever.

For more than two weeks his condition deteriorated. Finally, he died in his bed.

Local burial customs call for a two-day wake in the home of the deceased. Meanwhile, no one was sure where Rosa was or how to contact her. In those days there were a few phones but no cell phones and no pagers. Furthermore, most villagers had no need to speak to people from other rural areas. So the local church people prayed that God would speak to Rosa and instruct her to come home.

The two-day wake passed and it was time to bury the young man. Still there was no word from Rosa or knowledge of her whereabouts. In fact, she could have been hundreds of miles away because she went from place to place as instructed by the Holy Spirit. The daughter-in-law said they should wait one more day for Rosa to come and see her son before they buried him. Again the day passed with no sign of Rosa.

The family continued to wait because Rosa was elderly and they wanted her to see her only son one last time so she could say an appropriate good-bye. That was understandable. But Angelo had now been dead three days and without the benefit of embalming it was absolutely necessary to bury him fairly quickly.

On the fourth day, everyone agreed that her son would be buried that afternoon even if Rosa hadn't returned. Shortly after lunchtime, however, Rosa disembarked from one of the rusty, dented buses. Angelo had been wrapped in burial clothes and the family was awaiting the village burial crew to take him to his final resting place. But his body was still in Rosa's house.

When Rosa arrived home she was not gripped by grief at the sight of her dead son. All the families were wailing, but not Rosa! She asked everyone to leave the room. The family and friends slowly passed by and went outside. Someone asked her how long it would be before she released Angelo's body for burial.

Rosa responded robustly, "There will be no burial. My son will live again." How could she make such a remark? He had been dead three-and-a-half days. But it was simple! Rosa had dedicated Angelo to God and to the work of the ministry. She was certain he was called to preach and had not yet fulfilled his calling. Therefore, he could not stay dead because his time was not yet fulfilled on the earth.

After everyone was outside, Rosa went to the room where Angelo's body lay wrapped in grave clothes. She closed the door and told her daughter-in-law she was not coming out until God resurrected her son. She believed demon powers had killed him, and now she was going to attack them and win her son back in Jesus' name.

For a long season there was no sound but the voice of Rosa praying. And then the voice of Angelo was heard saying softly, "What day is this? I feel like I have been asleep for days." His wife ran in with great rejoicing, and quickly other friends and family joined in joy. In a few minutes the entire village was full of the news of a great miracle. A wake had been converted into a revival.

At the time of our lunch together, Angelo had been pastoring for two years. He was healthy and strong and constantly gave God praise for his life—now given to him twice. Jesus said, "I am the resurrection and the life" (John 11:25).

Paul confirms that same idea by stating, "But if there is no resurrection from the dead, not even Christ has been raised" (1 Corinthians 15:13). That is our hope!

Chapter 13

GRAVE DISCOVERY

Author's note:

Some of the things one sees and hears while traveling are a bit hard for a Western-mindset person to accept and believe. By contrast, many people across the world readily believe in supernatural phenomena, demons, angels, and so on. They also believe that the world of the supernatural invades daily life at many intersections. This story is another from Peru where ancient tribes have a long history of engaging the "powers."

Peru has an ancient, highly-developed system of religion and an extensive road and postal system. A large number of ruins and recovered artifacts bear evidence to this. An American missionary in that country asked if our team would like to see some of the ancient ruins and cultural displays. "Yes," we answered, and a plan was made.

Two hours out of Lima we visited a restored village and cultural center built on the edge of an ancient Indian burial ground. The tribe that had occupied this area had extensive skills in metalworking and jewelry making. Hence, many artifacts had been found there intact and perfectly preserved. A few of lesser consequence were in the cultural center for viewing, and most of the rest were in the national museum in Lima. Other pieces were in museums around the world.

The cultural center leads to a short path, at the end of which is the main street of a restored ancient village. Various staffers, dressed in authentic historical costumes, worked at skills as they would have been had they lived many centuries before. Some made pottery while others created jewelry and metal pieces faithful to ancient designs. One highlight for me was dining at a small restaurant that claimed it served food cooked from ancient recipes. (I will not comment here on the consequences of eating there.)

Near the end of the three-block-long main street was a large, locked iron gate, overseen by a sleepy-eyed guard. I asked him what was beyond the gate since the pathway turned and I could not see any farther. The guard answered, "The spirits of the dead are out there. They do not want to be disturbed, so we keep people from wandering around in their territory." As I peered through the gate rungs, I saw what looked like a vast plain that been committed to burial places. But little could be clearly seen from where we stood.

We learned in a lecture at the cultural center that the ancients buried their dead in a fetal position but sitting up. They were buried in holes in the ground shaped like olive oil bottles. The corpses were placed in the holes on their bottoms. From a side view it appeared that a person sat down, put his head between his knees and pulled his legs up around his ears. The tops of the holes were not more than one foot across. I am still wondering how the corpses were placed inside. It is a ship-in-a-bottle type mystery wherein a stone shaped like a bottle cork is fitted for the opening.

The guard seemed chilly towards the idea of letting us wander among the "spirits," so we ambled back through the village. We were struck by the perceived need to protect the sites, but our hearts had not been particularly set to look at burial sites anyway.

Our host, a chap named William, said very little, but in a few minutes he led us back to the gate. He mentioned to the guard that we were "spiritual people," that we respected the dead and their history, and he offered a small "offering" in their memory. The words and coin worked. Shortly, we were looking at a burial ground covering more than 1,000 acres.

There were no roads or even well-worn walking paths and we had to be careful not to step into any of the hundreds of open grave holes. The openings were about as large as my foot when it is planted flat down. They were everywhere and as far as we could see. It was from these burial grounds that so many artifacts, jewelry and metal pieces, have been found. This ancient tribe buried personal jewelry and riches in the grave with the deceased.

The overall site was something like a moonscape. No trees, grass, or bushes of any kind could be seen. Grainy, reddish sand was everywhere. We walked up a slight incline and noticed we were atop a hill that had a cliff side about forty feet high. This cliff side was full of grave holes dug laterally. Our sleepy guard-guide said that the priests were buried in that area, the high places, so they could "look over" the souls of the departed.

It was in observing that cliff that we came into direct contact with the spirit realm. We could all hear sounds of a deep, low-toned, quiet sighing. The sound was akin to wind blowing through treetops. At first, I reckoned the sounds to be some physical phenomenon, but there was nothing physically present to produce them. So I said nothing until one of the ladies said, "I think I'm hearing things." With nervous laughter all six of us acknowledged the same. The spirit world related to the dead was disturbed that we Christians were there on their territory. We stood together, joined hands, and asked God for protection. The sighing sounds did not stop, but our fears did in an instant.

We wandered around a good while and finally relocated the path leading back to the gate and village. All the way back we walked in the grainy red sand. Every step taken sounded like breaking glass when our feet pressed down to walk. Once through the gate, the sounds of glass breaking and the sighings stopped.

The guard looked at us, his facial expression and voice showing he was obviously upset. Sweating profusely he said, "Go out quickly. The gods are disturbed and the spirits have been stirred up. You must go quickly." We picked up the pace to the car park and immediately left the premises. We did not leave because of fear; we left in respect of the ancient traditions and in deference to the guard who had been reckless with his responsibilities for a small tip.

We learned anew that day that there *is* a spirit realm and that realm is as real as the one we have contact with through our senses. There are real demon powers, and we had stepped into territory they had long claimed for themselves. We were reminded also, however, that there is—above and beyond—Jesus Christ who is the Ruler above all principalities and powers. It is a good thing to serve and know Him.

Chapter 14

MEXICAN MURDERERS TRANSFORMED

M any times we have led teams into Mexico for evangelism in towns and villages. Because many churches send teams to work along the border, we chose to take our teams deeper into the interior of the country. The setting for this story is a coastal town on the Pacific side of Mexico, about 800 miles south of the U. S. border. It is a picturesque town built on terraces overlooking the sea. Ten days of ministry were planned for this town.

Our primary focus was on a part of town well known for its crime and poverty. Expensive villas overlooked the seas. But the area where we planned to work had tin shanties, no running water, and no public sanitation system. What it did have was crime, prostitution, drugs, shootings, and stabbings—all with regularity. Alcoholism was rampant. Because of the social issues, most of the villagers lived below the poverty line.

Those who worked, worked for the wealthy, and seeing their excesses fueled intense hatred in the shantytown. Attendance in school was so irregular that teachers had difficulty completing courses so students could pass comprehensive exams. Students did not attend enough classes to learn the material. When they did decide to attend school, some arrived drunk while others were exhausted from lack of sleep because of loud, late-night partying in their neighborhood.

Our Mexican friend Joel thought this town would be a great place to preach and plant a church. We agreed. "Where sin abounds, grace abounds much more." The darkest places respond first to light.

The conditions brought with them a certain level of risk for our team. Most of our female team members were blondes. And Americans were hated there as they are in many places around the world. Yet, the reason to go is because Jesus loves all people.

When our team arrived four hours later than anticipated, we were directed to a small hotel on the beachfront. It was 11:30 P.M. and the hotel disco rocked with loud music and the laughter of people drinking. This was not a special night of celebration. The partying was part of the life of the town and went on every night with varying degrees of debauchery. The disco closed when the last person departed, which was usually five or six o'clock in the morning.

Our team was subdivided into smaller teams consisting of at least one male and one Spanish speaker, plus as many others as was practical. Usually a team was four to six persons. Teams of that size could subdivide and cover both sides of a street going house-to-house or gather together if several people wanted to talk about Jesus. Many times teenagers could be gathered together and good conversations about Jesus followed.

Each group was equipped with literature, an invitation to the evening services, and candy for the children in each house. Most homes received the teams well. A few had placards stating, "No evangelistic literature accepted," so we left none except the invitation to the services. All day long until 4 P.M. the teams worked. They gathered for prayer from 5:30–7:30 P.M. and the service followed.

Joel had moved to town six months before our team arrived. A garden plot dug out of the side of the mountain had been donated for a church site—a small terrace on a rocky outcropping overlooking the ocean. Joel had started a small church after he had built two small rooms for his family to live in as temporary housing. The church walls had been completed to about six feet in height, but there were no windows, floor, or roof. That partially finished place is where services were held. Electricity was supplied from a power cord running from a nearby house.

Music is always an attention-getter, and that was no exception here. Our team was multitalented in vocal and instrumental music. At service time we began to play and sing. The neighbors assumed it was another party and, within a few minutes, the church grounds were completely full. People were sitting atop the unfinished walls and in the open window areas. Those were dangerous places to perch because if a person fell out, he or she would go straight down the slope and into the ocean.

The band played and got the people to engage in a sing-a-long. Some songs were sung in Spanish while others were used to teach the people to sing in English. The crowd was won by the music. Some of the men asked for *chicha*, the local alcoholic drink made from corn. A few left angrily when they were told none would be available.

The gospel was preached and no one responded. The message of Jesus Christ was presented a second time because the speaker thought the people did not understand. Again, no one responded. The band and singers sang a few more songs and then the people were dismissed. Some young people engaged our team in conversation, but none expressed a desire to accept the Lord.

Several days and nights of services passed. Houses were visited, people were talked to, people came to church, but none responded to the preaching of the gospel of Jesus. An extra hour of prayer was added in the mornings, but otherwise the daily routine remained the same.

Saturday night the change came in an unusual way. The service had gone as the others had—with one difference. On this glorious night three people accepted Christ. Many others lingered around till 1:30 A.M. Team members explained the gospel and its importance to them over and over again. As the night went along, a few more asked Christ into their lives. A small breakthrough was finally happening. We did not know it then, but an even greater miracle was in the making.

On the mountainside above the church, many families were building houses on the slopes. Some of those people had a direct view down and into the church. One house had a view into one half of the church as well as into the section where the platform was to be constructed. No roof or windows had been built on the church yet, so the people on the slopes could both see and hear.

On top of one of the houses two men were sitting drinking beer. Both were contract killers. Murder for hire was their business, and they were the most feared men in the entire area. Some locals reported that twenty-two people had been killed by these men, but there was never any proof as the people they killed had been thrown into the sea and eaten by sharks. Pastor Joel had warned our team not to visit in the area around that house, but he had not explained why.

At 2:00 that morning, these two men climbed the path down to the church and wanted to speak to Pastor Joel. They were both well on the way to being drunk. When they arrived, everyone in the church left quickly with eyes down and heads bowed. Our group was given the signal to leave as well. Little did we know that after we left, the two men—with pistols tucked in their belts—would ask the pastor to tell them about God.

The conversation lasted till 5:30 A.M. They explained to the pastor that they had seen a light over the top of the church in the shape of a high cross. At first they thought it was the effects of alcohol. But the next night it was there again. The foot of the cross appeared to be standing at the altar area of the new church. After seeing this cross for five nights, they decided this must be a sign from God. As a result, in fear, they came to see the pastor. After long discussions, both men knelt and received Christ as Savior.

The village people were amazed the next night when the men were back in church with their guns, but not drunk, mean, or threatening. They knelt again and publicly prayed for forgiveness. Others in the church had difficulty believing what they were seeing.

Three days later our team headed for home. I often wondered what happened to those two men. Later I learned that some months after they received Christ, the pastor took them to the police to confess their crimes. Before they could tell their stories, the police chief stood up and said, "We have seen such a change in your lives we cannot believe it."

Since being converted, the two men ran off pimps, drug dealers, and illegal alcohol dealers from the town. They also donated a piece of land for a children's park and worked hard to help finish the church. Best of all, there were no more killings. The police chief asked these new converts if they would go on a tour from town to town to tell others what had happened to them.

In subsequent years one of the men became a pastor. The other became an evangelist and worked among Indian and native tribes in Southern Mexico.

It's amazing what can be seen from a housetop. King David saw a young woman, desired her, and had her husband killed to get her. His gaze produced death and misery. The Mexican murderers saw a church service, heard the gospel in song and word, and the result in their lives was salvation and blessing. Wisdom would say, be careful where you gaze.

Chapter 15

A CHURCH BEGUN IN ONE DAY

A large church in California assembled a ministry group gleaned from among several churches to hold a crusade in Mexico. Logistical support was difficult because the group totaled more than 100 persons, traveling by bus, cars, and vans. Where to sleep? Where to prepare food? How could the sound equipment and baggage be handled? Large groups create large challenges.

For about ten days the ministry team carried on the crusade with good success. Crowds were large, people responded, and the ministry team stayed healthy and well. Day sixteen of the twenty-one day trip was planned as a day off. The team was staying in a beach community and everyone was ready for a day of rest and recreation. Some were on the beach, some were shopping, some sleeping, and others just hanging out relaxing.

I chose the beach because it was hot and humid, and the water was refreshing. The beach offered good relief. Two other team members joined me in a quiet spot to swim, sunbathe, and read.

At mid-afternoon, a young member who had driven his own car on the mission appeared on the beach. John was fluent in several languages including Spanish. He had not been shopping or swimming. He had been traveling some sandy trails thirty to fifty miles from where we were ministering.

There was urgency on his face and in his voice. "Brother Dale, there is a miracle in the making," he said excitedly. "You must come with me to the place now that I just visited. There is a man there you must speak with."

John's words came fast, were passionate and repetitive. I protested a bit, telling him to calm down, that he should be resting. But John would not take no for an answer. He continued to insist on an immediate trip to a village thirty-five miles away down a rutted sand path. He suggested we go there in his car, a new, low-slung American model. I wondered if I agreed to go, would we even make it?

Finally, I surrendered to John's request, walked back to the hotel, changed my clothes, and joined him in his car for the bumpy ride. He did not slow down because of the poor road conditions. Did I use the word road? That's an overstatement.

Words of faith and excitement poured out of John the entire way. "There is a miracle in the making. This is incredible. You are not going to believe it." In truth, I was not looking for a miracle that day—only sunshine, water, and rest.

We drove through muddy holes, flocks of sheep, people walking between towns, around wandering cows and horses, and greeted cowboys with guns slung over their shoulders. Finally we arrived in the village of El Montana. It looked like a hundred other small towns and villages I have been in across the world. The people were poor. Subsistence farms surrounded the town that had a mid-town square typical of Mexican culture. Everyone and everything moved slowly. That is the pace of life in a village—slow!

John drove around the square to find a man sitting on the wooden curb. There were no concrete sidewalks, only plank walkways like one would see in an old Western movie. We drove up to a young man seated alone. John said, "That's him—Peter. That's the guy with the miracle." Through my tired eyes it looked like anything but a miracle. We got out of the car and sat on either side of the man.

Immediately John pressed Peter, "Tell him. Tell him about the miracle. Tell him about the vision."

I must confess. Here we were in a pitifully poor village using a perfectly wonderful beach day to make the visit. And we had departed from an ultramodern ocean front hotel. This was not fun so far. There were no streets, just lots of dust and sand trails. It was hot, and El Montana was not on our schedule. I wanted to get back to the beach.

But that was not to be. God's plans are always bigger, better, and different from ours. Peter began to share what had happened in his life. Briefly it was this. He was an unbeliever; only one believer lived in the town. That person was an elderly lady who spent her days in prayer and counseling young mothers. She owned various properties. During a period of illness, she had hired Peter, who was trained as a carpenter, to do some work for her on her home. On one of these work assignments, she led Peter to faith in

Christ. She also said, "God has his hand on you for ministry and greatness."

That was beyond his wildest dream. Ministry? Peter the carpenter? How could this be? When would this come to pass?

Two weeks after accepting Christ, Peter had a vision in which he saw things that amazed him. He saw himself as pastor of a church on the town square of El Montana. At the time there was no possibility of that happening. He also saw a group of Americans in his vision. To his knowledge no groups of Americans had ever visited the town. Why should they?

Peter heard the voice of the Lord telling him to do three things. First, prepare a building for a church. Second, pray for the Americans to come. Third, study the Bible every day. Two of the three were easy. He could study the Bible, and he had to wait for the Americans. But what about securing and preparing a building?

The building was the greatest challenge. How could one be secured, especially for a congregation not yet in existence? Half of the store buildings around the town square were empty. El Montana was a poor place. Once a week Peter prayed with the elderly lady who had led him to Christ. After being visited with the same vision three times, he shared it with his friend. She confirmed it was from the Lord.

Peter said, "I don't know what to do about a building." The woman grinned. She owned several of the buildings on the square and immediately donated one for a church.

Town rules required that all building fronts remain in old architectural style, but the interiors could be modernized. As time and money were available, Peter remodeled one store into a church. He built new walls, benches, an altar, and prayer rails. After three years it was finished.

I asked, "Where is this place?"

Peter responded, "It's right behind you." We went inside, and there before us was a beautiful chapel that would seat 120 persons. That, by itself, was a miracle.

"How many people attend this church?" I asked Peter. "None yet," he replied. "We don't have a congregation yet."

"When are you going to get one?" I asked.

"When the Americans come and hold services in the town square. After that we will have a congregation."

Frankly this story was getting harder to believe all the time. I pressed Peter all the more. "Do you mean you have been waiting for an American evangelism team to launch a church in this village in one day?"

"Yes," he said. "That is what God told me."

What should we do? What could we do? Our team was scattered all over town, the shops, and the beach, and that was our only day of rest. But it was now very clear to me that we were being swept into something long in planning in the heart of God. He was engineering something beyond our experience levels, something we had never seen before, and something we were having trouble believing.

I told Peter some of us would be back that night for a service in the town square. I could not promise a big team, since I was quite sure we could not find everyone. John and I headed back to town and found about half the group around the hotel. We told them briefly what had transpired and asked for volunteers to be part of an evening event. Forty or so people decided to go. We loaded the bus with musical instruments and people and set off for El Montana. Traveling there with that big bus was not easy, but we eventually arrived in town.

Half the team was assigned set-up duties; the other half stayed on the bus with me to intercede for the service. Excitement began to grow in my heart. We were going to be part of something really good the Lord had designed. I began to anticipate miracles.

As the sun was setting, people gathered by the dozens. The Americans were a spectacle to see, and why were they here? What kind of music did they play? What was this about? The band began to play and yet more people came. A large amount of the music had been memorized in Spanish and the town people loved hearing it in their own language.

We faced a few challenges. One opposition group sent a band of people through the crowd beating drums, and drunk cowboys rode horses through the crowd shooting rifles. But the crowd could not be intimidated and would not leave the square. Thankfully, no one was injured.

God gave me grace to speak about Jesus and His love for people. At the end of the message about 500 adults came around to the front of the stage to accept Christ as Savior. Many were also healed, including the mayor's sister. She had a tumor so large she appeared to be in the last stages of pregnancy. After a few minutes of prayer, her dress, which had been taut, was hanging loose on her. By the end of the evening she could wrap the dress fabric around her body twice. It was a visible and amazing healing.

From the large group that responded to the invitation to accept Christ as Savior, a church congregation rose up that very day. We introduced Peter as the new pastor. Applause broke out because many people knew him, and they knew him to be a man of integrity. Between eighty and one hundred adults formed the new church that started in a day.

Did this event qualify as a miracle? Our teams thought so. The people of El Montana thought so. What do you think?

PART FOUR:

Miracles in America

Chapter 16

MEDICINE MAN'S MIRACLE

A large urban church had missions in its heart and in the center of its ministry expressions. Staffing the local downtown soup kitchen, constructing houses for the poor in Third World nations, and digging water wells in Africa were only a few of its ministries. One year a combination of an adult Sunday school class and the youth department agreed to go on a mission trip to east-central Arizona.

The mission was planned over the Christmas holidays, but none of the normal touches of Christmas had visited the Native American reservation. The landscape was barren, covered with red rocks and red dirt.

The plan called for building construction during the day and church services in the evening. Advertising had gone out for weeks that a musical group would perform at church every night.

All the normal negatives of reservation life were present. Broken and abandoned cars sat near almost every house.

The houses were in various states of disrepair with broken and unhinged doors, a lack of paint, and an abundance of trash and debris. The nearest city was sixty miles away, and a small town of 400 inhabitants was forty miles away.

The mission station was one of the brighter spots in the area. It had no trash heaps, no broken doors and windows, no abandoned cars. Most of the buildings were in good condition. The yards had been watered, planted, and tended. A well had been drilled a year earlier, so there was running water in some of the buildings. But septic tanks were not possible because of the rocky soil. The toilets were in a little shed a few yards behind the church. The mission station also had a few trees, a rarity in those parts.

Everyone slept on the floor in the church. Meals were prepared in the church kitchen. Showers were the end of a garden hose, and it was cold enough to snow a few inches. Locally, all the normal social problems were present, especially alcoholism. In one place empty and broken liquor bottles were heaped in a pile two stories high. Even young children were seen drinking, and many were drunk daily. There were numerous stories of child and spousal abuse. It was not safe to visit in most homes because of these alcohol and abuse problems.

With no gainful employment on the reservation itself, the people survived on government-funded handouts and welfare. They were poor in spirit and body, environmentally, financially, and spiritually.

Various programs had been organized for children, but few youngsters could be found. Those who could be found were extremely shy. Most children huddled on the porches of their houses and not beyond. Occasionally one or two would speak up and respond, but that was rare.

Members of the ministry team went daily around the reservation, handing out invitations, and nailing up advertisements. Others tried to go from house to house, but almost no one invited them in or promised to come to a service. Most noticeable to the team was the sadness on the people's faces. After two days of resistance, the group spent additional hours in prayer for the people they had seen.

Three night meetings were planned consisting of ninety percent music and a short sermon, followed by an invitation to receive Christ. The first night the building was half full at the beginning and packed at the end. The second night the building was jammed from the beginning, and halfway through, people were standing around the inside walls. This meeting was destined to be powerful and unusual.

Near the end of the gospel presentation, the speaker addressed a Native American man who was standing next to the rear exit door. He was well on his way to being drunk. The speaker addressed him and said, "Sir, I believe you have stomach problems. Please come to the front so I can pray with you." Slowly the man made his way around the side aisle to the front.

While he was slowly making his way through the crowded side aisles, the speaker continued to observe him. He heard the Holy Spirit whisper, "This man is demon possessed. Pray and expel the demons from him; do not touch him in any way."

When the man was positioned directly in front of the speaker, he began to shake and tremble. The speaker told the audience, "This man is demon-possessed, and I am going to cast the demons out of him now."

Upon that announcement, the room was hushed. People strained to see, and some stood on their seats. Many grasped the person next to them in fear, while others shut their eyes so they could not see what was happening. Why was there such a dramatic reaction in the crowd? Because—*The man being prayed for was the local medicine man who had kept everyone in fear with his curses, fetishes, and incantations.*

Now the medicine man stood shaking like a reed in the wind. He was mute and unable to speak a word. When the speaker gave the command for the demons to leave, the man fell on the floor in a deathlike trance. Many in the audience began to cry in fear. Weeping was an unusual expression in their culture.

After some minutes the medicine man revived and was helped to his feet. He asked for a translator since he understood most English but spoke none. He then testified that he was free, truly free, for the first time in his life. A smile spread across his face.

The speaker invited him to the stage where he gave a lengthier testimony to his people. He said he had possessed no power but fear. He admitted he kept the people in fear to control them and to get money, but confessed that his magic did not work. With that testimony in their ears, the entire church began to shout and clap.

The speaker then invited all others who wanted to be free to come and receive Christ as Savior. They did so by the dozens. The altar service and prayer counseling went on till late in the evening.

Because of this incredible event, the ministry team decided it would be profitable to stay two additional days. The next day some of the team members went to the grocery store for milk and bread. When they came to the checkout counter, the clerk appeared very nervous.

In broken English he asked, "Are you the God people who hold meeting at mission station?"

"Yes," they responded.

The clerk bagged the groceries and said, "Go, no pay . . . you too powerful to pay for grocery, so go. God wants you to have them."

The next two days and nights were full of counseling, prayer, soul winning, and relationship building. People came to the mission station all day long to inquire about spiritual matters. The medicine man was also there all day, apologizing to people for the things he had done to them and their families and asking for forgiveness. The resident missionaries said they had never seen a response like the one the Lord was producing through the young people.

The final night people came from as far away as 200 miles. Family members had phoned about the powerful demonstration of God and came to see what was happening. The presence of God was so strong people came to the altar to repent even before the service began.

What happened? Satan had held the medicine man in his grip, and through him the people came into spiritual darkness and bondage. Today, the medicine man is the assistant pastor at the mission station. What a great deliverance!

One should be careful whom they follow. Is your leader taking you to deeper places in your spiritual walk? Are you a better person and more in love with Jesus by following the persons to whom you have submitted your spiritual life? It is a good thing to consider.

Chapter 17

JAILHOUSE
JUBILATION

Prison, the can, the lockup, the clink, the hoosegow—all are names for a place where freedom-loving people do not want to reside. Jail is for those who have broken the law; at least that is the case in our land.

In other countries people are often unjustly imprisoned for political and/or religious reasons. Jails come in many sizes and varieties, from local town holding cells to maximum-security federal prisons. Somewhere in the middle of the severity list are the county jails, usually located in the center of large metropolitan areas. Cook County Jail, for instance, is in downtown Chicago. Harris County jail is in Houston.

Many churches have ministries in all the prison levels mentioned above. This story is about a county jail, a church ministry group, and an outpouring of the Holy Spirit that no one expected. It should encourage your faith to believe that God can work in such unusual ways and places.

At one church, Monday nights were designated jail ministry night. A group of fifteen usually made up the visitation team. Upon arrival at the county jail, the team was broken into smaller groups of five so ministry could be conducted on three floors simultaneously. The county jail had six floors, and each floor had a service lasting about an hour. A person in each group led in worship and played a guitar. Others gave testimonies, and one person was designated to present the gospel, followed by an invitation to receive Christ as Savior.

This prison ministry had gone on for years and many had been touched. But this particular county jail was a rough place in which to minister. It was a holding jail where prisoners were held until their cases could be heard, and they were then sent to other appropriate institutions to complete their sentence. All the incarcerated were thrown in together from murderers to men failing to pay child support.

The church ministry groups were accepted by some, cursed by others, and treated passively by yet others. At a minimum, the singing and preaching provided a time-filling distraction. Yet, God worked in the midst of this raucous atmosphere.

One night, like hundreds of other Monday nights, the prison ministry team prayed together on the jailhouse steps and went in for the normal searches and security checks. After being admitted, they broke into teams and headed to the various floors to share the gospel. After ministering on all six floors, the team reassembled in the foyer and went home. It seemed like a normal evening.

Then at 3 A.M. the phone ran in the home of Jill and Al, the team leaders. On the line was the county sheriff who was responsible for the county prison. Al picked up the phone. When he heard the sheriff, he sat straight up in bed and asked, "What's happening?"

The sheriff shared a strange report, along with an unusual request. It seems that two hours after the ministry team had left the jail, weeping and repentance had broken out among the prisoners on every floor. This had been going on for hours. Prisoners were singing and others rejoicing after they had confessed their crimes and sins. So many prisoners were confessing, the sheriff did not know what to do, and at that late hour, not many lawyers were excited about going downtown to see their clients.

The sheriff told Al, "In all my twenty-eight years in law enforcement, I have never seen anything like this, and I don't know what to do about it. Even the jail guards are crying. The prison is out of control. This breakout of religion is the direct consequence of your religious activity, and I need your help to get it back under control." He asked Al if the department sent a lady to look after their children, would he and Jill come back to the jail and help settle the prisoners down. They agreed to go.

Back at the jail, Al and Jill could not believe what was happening. Prisoners on every floor were singing, some praising the Lord with hands raised, others crying out in anguish of heart and confessing their sins and crimes to God (and later to lawyers and judges). Hundreds of people, both prisoners and jail personnel, were under the influence of the presence of God. The scene looked like a classical revival service from olden times, but this was the county jail.

As soon as Al and Jill saw the enormity of the situation, they called others from their team to come and assist. Literally hundreds of people were coming to Christ and needed counsel and help. The jail revival went on all night and into the next morning. Finally things settled down a bit and the workers went home.

Within two hours the sheriff called to say that there had been another outbreak and he needed help. The local newspapers heard the rumors and rushed over to see for themselves what was happening. The next day the jail revival was front page news highlighted with a headline that read, "Holy Roller Religion Hits Jailhouse." This jailhouse revival of religion went on for a total of seven weeks, night and day. Hundreds of prisoners were transformed during those weeks.

Three years later Jill heard a knock on her front door and opened it to a door-to-door salesman. As soon as he saw Jill's face he began to cry.

"I don't believe it," he said. "I don't believe it. This is too wonderful to be true."

Jill asked, "Sir, what are you talking about?"

He responded, "Ma'am, did you hold services in the county jail some years ago?" Jill responded in the affirmative. The salesman said, "I was one of those prisoners listening when you preached. My life was completely changed that night. I was in jail for passing bad checks. Now I have paid everything back, my record is clean, and I am serving Jesus. I am a Christian because of your jail ministry. Thank you, thank you, thank you in Jesus' name."

This salesman was just one of hundreds who were challenged and changed during the seven weeks God moved in power at the jailhouse. As said elsewhere, God is truly at work!

Chapter 18

OUT OF THE CLOSET

The setting is a plain, non-descript town in Middle America shortly after World War II, located in an area usually dubbed "the grain belt." Life in such towns moves slowly and is defined by the seasons of sowing, cultivating, and harvesting. This town is named after a German family called Maybach who settled in the area many years before.

Shortly after World War II, a Pentecostal evangelist had been conducting tent crusades in mid-America. These meetings had taken place from April to September to take advantage of the warm weather. A small team of dedicated workers traveled with the evangelist. They worked at everything from truck driving, to raising and lowering the tent, to conducting music and altar prayers. It was hot, hard work, but rewarding because people came to Christ almost every night.

For several years, evangelist James had crisscrossed his state and those nearby with tent crusades. In a season of fasting and prayer, the name Maybach kept coming to him and stayed in his thoughts almost daily. He did not know what the name meant, but thought it might be a town. He also had a sense that the place was in his home state although he had never heard of it.

The instructions of the Lord were clear: James was to go there and preach. He visited library after library and reviewed the best maps without success. Maybach was nowhere to be found. It was puzzling. For three years the name Maybach stayed in his thoughts and prayers, but he did not know how to find the place. He kept increasing his prayers about this matter, because he felt such a strong leading from the Lord.

Nearly three years after receiving his first impression about Maybach, evangelist James and his team were having lunch in a café in a small town while on their way to another location for a crusade. James happened to ask the waitress if she had ever heard of Maybach.

To his amazement she said, "Yes, it's only fifteen miles from here."

James was shocked that this information was so easily gained after three years of searching. The obvious question that followed was, "Why is that place not on any maps?"

With a sneer on her face and disgust in her voice she said, "They're ashamed. It's full of homosexuals and perverts, and the politicians are so ashamed they refuse to put the city on any state map or acknowledge its existence." No wonder Evangelist James had been burdened in prayer for the place. Plans were immediately made for a tent crusade there the next summer.

Throughout the winter prior to the crusade in Maybach, intercessors prayed daily for a breakthrough in that town. The environment of the Maybach meeting would be unlike any the evangelist had encountered before. But when the time came, permits were granted easily enough and up went the tent. The population was a mixture of gays, sexual perverts of various kinds, and non-gays. There was a general buzz about the tent preacher coming to town and having the audacity to preach in Maybach. Everyone knew nothing could be done in that unholy place.

Or could it? Certainly dozens of people were curious enough to visit the tent.

James had decided that Maybach was so low spiritually and its condition so bad he would spend the entire summer there. After three weeks of stiff resistance, people began receiving Christ in large numbers, and that was the beginning of a breakthrough. All around town residents were talking about the tent meetings, about God, and how lives were beginning to change.

Summer came to an end and it had been spiritually profitable. James was leaving town by train on September 2 to go to a speaking engagement in another state. As he was walking from the guesthouse where he had been staying, the new pastor he had appointed in town began to walk along with him.

"There is a lady who wants to see you just for a few moments before you leave," he told James. "Her house is on the way to the station and she won't keep you long." Since there was a half hour to spare, James agreed to a brief visit.

"Here's the house," said the pastor. Behind a slightly warped screen door stood a small lady with a notable head of white hair. Before James and the pastor could mount the front steps, she had invited them inside.

"My name is Adellane," she introduced herself. "I am 76 years old and have lived all my life in Maybach. I was born, raised, and married in this house, and I've never been out of the county in my entire life." With that she said, "Come here" as she headed for the back of her house, her small hand waving her guests to join her in the kitchen. Tea and cookies had been prepared.

As she handed a box of baked goodies to James, she said, "There is something I want to show you." She opened her broom closet. There he saw a kneeling pad, a short bench, and her worn Bible. "This is my prayer closet," she said.

Then the rest of her story tumbled out. "In my sixteenth year I was married. Also, that year, a Free Methodist itinerant evangelist came to town. After receiving Christ in his meetings, I felt a great need to pray for my town and, later, for my children and relatives. Since I was 16 years old I have used this closet for a prayer chamber." She looked with great fondness into the closet while turning the door handle back and forth.

Adellane continued, "I have prayed here two hours a day, seven days a week for the last sixty years. God promised me that one day before I died He would send someone to again preach the gospel here. This summer, seventy-seven friends and relatives have found Christ as Savior. I can go home now because you have come and God has fulfilled his promise."

James and the pastor could hardly speak through their tears. Imagine . . . sixty years of prayer alone in a closet praying for one town. How could one woman stay in the grip of God, burdened and resolute all those years? Alone. Those who pray do hold the world together.

The breakthrough in Maybach was not from good preaching and uplifting music. Breakthrough came as a result of a faithful praying woman who labored behind a closed door, day in and day out for sixty years. May her tribe increase!

$\mathscr{C}h\ a\ p\ t\ e\ r$ 19

THE LAST WORD

A personal word from the author:

I sincerely hope you have enjoyed the stories I've shared and that you have been strengthened and encouraged by them. The events you have read happened in various countries across a time span covering many years.

Taken together, these stories report loudly and clearly that there are significant signs of a living God who is working in the world *today*. These reports should upgrade your faith a notch.

God has been working all over the world, in every nation, in extravagantly large numbers of ways, and in many people groups. From the steel-glass towers of metropolitan centers to yurts on central Asian steppes, to hovels in Hyderabad, I have seen signs of His life and work.

The stories you have read are a miniscule part of His story. They provide a mere glimpse of His passion for people, of the universality of the Good News, and of the extent to which God will go to let a person know that He is, that He is good, and that He personally cares.

My personal wish

When a rainy day of discouragement deposits all sorts of negativity and distress in your life, I pray that you will reread a chapter or two of this book and follow with an honest outpouring of your feelings and heart to God. Then reread Hebrews chapter 11 slowly and reflectively. Ask God to step into your life personally, powerfully, and passionately.

Many witnesses to God's greatness are recorded in this book. These stories are from real people in real life situations. Some of the situations were difficult to the extreme, but the believers had success because of their relationship with Jesus.

My family and I join their collective witness to the greatness of God by testifying that, on a personal level and through many years of living in both good and bad times, we have trusted God and He has not failed us. Not once! You can trust Him, too!

To order additional copies of

MIRACLES
Around the
Globe

Have your credit card ready and call:

1-877-421-READ (7323)

or please visit our web site at
www.pleasantword.com

Also available at: www.amazon.com

Printed in the United States
21142LVS00001B/214-279